Sean McManus

Scratch
Programming

in
easy steps

Second Edition
updated for Scratch 3

In easy steps is an imprint of In Easy Steps Limited
16 Hamilton Terrace · Holly Walk · Leamington Spa
Warwickshire · United Kingdom · CV32 4LY
www.ineasysteps.com

Notice of Liability

Trademarks

In Easy Steps Limited supports The Forest Stewardship Council (FSC), the leading international forest certification organization. All our titles that are printed on Greenpeace approved FSC certified paper carry the FSC logo.

MIX
Paper from
responsible sources
FSC® C020837

Printed and bound in the United Kingdom

ISBN 978-1-84078-859-4

Contents

1 Introducing Scratch

In this chapter, you'll get started with Scratch, including meeting some of the blocks used to give instructions, and creating your first program. You'll also learn how to save your work, and load projects created by others.

Scratch doesn't cost anything and it works on Windows, Mac and Linux computers, as well as tablet devices. For the latest version of Scratch, the Raspberry Pi Foundation recommends a Raspberry Pi 4 computer (pictured below) with at least 2GB of RAM.

Above: A simple Scratch program, showing how the color-coded commands lock together.

What is Scratch?

Programming is the art of writing instructions to tell a computer what to do. A set of instructions is called a program. The instructions are written in what's known as a programming language, and there are thousands to choose from.

Scratch is a programming language that is perfect for making games, animations, interactive stories and other visually rich programs. It provides a great introduction to programming for people of all ages. It's widely used in schools and colleges, but Harvard University has also used it in higher education at its Summer School. I've led workshops for adults where Scratch provided a friendly introduction to the kind of creative problem solving that programmers do all the time.

Scratch is easier to use than most other programming languages for a number of reasons:

- You don't have to remember or type any commands: they're all on screen, so you can just drag and drop them.

- Commands fit together like jigsaw pieces, so there are strong visual hints about how you can combine them.

- Error messages are rare. Because Scratch commands lock together, programs usually make some kind of sense. It is possible to still write programs with logical errors in, if they don't do what you expected, but Scratch guides you to write things that work, rather than nagging you when they don't.

- The commands are color-coded and categorized, so you can easily find a command when you need it.

- The commands in Scratch simplify common activities in games, such as testing whether a missile has hit an alien (collision detection), or rotating a character on screen.

In short, Scratch is designed for your success. It enables you to quickly see results from your work, and even includes graphics and sounds you can use so you can get started right now. Many other programming languages require you to learn text commands, and have strict rules about how you can use them. Scratch doesn't. That means you can focus your energy instead on the fun stuff: dreaming up ideas for new programs, working out how to build them, designing them, and sharing them with friends.

Creating a Scratch account

Before you begin to program with Scratch, I recommend you create an account for the Scratch website. Here's how:

1 Open a web browser, such as Google Chrome

2 Enter the website address **https://scratch.mit.edu/** in your address bar, usually at the top of the screen

3 Click **Join Scratch** in the top right

4 Make up a username. The site advises you to protect your privacy by not using your real name. You can't change your username later, so choose wisely

5 Pick a password and enter it twice. The second time is to make sure you've typed it correctly. Use a mixture of uppercase and lowercase, numbers and symbols to make it more secure. Click the **Next** button

6 Enter your date of birth, gender, country and email address. This personal information is used to help you recover your password if you forget it, and is used by the Scratch team to understand who uses Scratch. Click **Next**

7 Enter an email address so they can confirm your account before you can share projects or post comments. Click **Next** and you will be logged in

The design of websites can change from time to time, so don't worry if you see variations in the sign-up process when you do it.

You can try Scratch by just going to the website and clicking Create at the top of the screen. If you use an account, though, the website will automatically save your work for you.

When you return to the site next time, you can click "Sign in" in the top right to get back to your projects.

Join Scratch

Your responses to these questions will be kept private.

Why do we ask for this info?

Birth Month and Year	- Month - ▼	- Year - ▼
Gender	○ Male ○ Female ○
Country	- Country - ▼

Next

Scratch 3 adds new features for making projects, a streamlined user interface, and compatibility with more devices.

Meet Scratch 3

Scratch 3 is the latest version of Scratch, launched in January 2019. It runs in your web browser and is based on standard web technologies (HTML5). That means it is compatible with many different types of computer. Scratch 3 introduced several new features, including:

● **Tablet support**. You can now build and use projects on a tablet device, and can play (but not build) projects on a mobile phone. Games that require keyboard controls to move a character on screen may not work. You can use your tablet's onscreen keyboard to type information into a project, though.

● **New extensions**. There are new capabilities to work with the micro:bit and Sense HAT devices, to speak out loud, to translate text, and to work with the Lego WeDo 2.0 and Lego Mindstorms EV3 kits. To add an extension, click the button in the bottom left of the screen.

● **Simplified Blocks Palette**. The menu of instructions has been streamlined by moving the music and drawing (Pen) blocks into the extensions section. If you're familiar with Scratch and are wondering where they went, you can find them there!

Older versions of Scratch (Scratch 2, and Scratch 1.4) are still available to download. There's an offline version of Scratch 3 too. Find them all at **https://scratch.mit.edu/download**

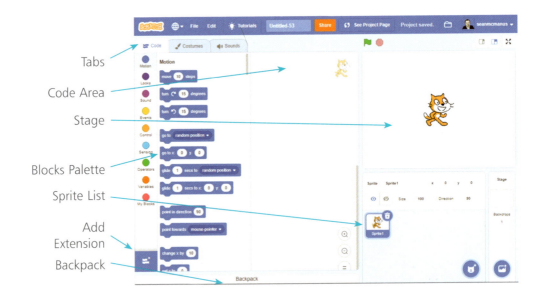

Tabs

Code Area

Stage

Blocks Palette

Sprite List

Add Extension

Backpack

Using the Scratch screen

The main parts of the Scratch screen, as shown on the facing page, are:

- **Stage**: This is where you can see your animations and games in action. When Scratch starts, there's a large orange cat in the middle of the Stage.

- **Sprite List**: The cat is a "sprite", which is like a character or object in a game. Your project might include lots of sprites, such as the player's spaceship, invading aliens and a missile. In the Sprite List, you can see all the sprites that are in your project, and click them to switch between them. The Sprite List is underneath the Stage.

- **Blocks Palette**: In Scratch, you give the computer commands by using blocks, which are instructions that fit together like jigsaw pieces. The Blocks Palette presents you with all the blocks you can use. When you start Scratch, you can see the Motion blocks, which are color-coded in dark blue, and are used for moving sprites around the Stage. You can browse a different set of blocks in the Blocks Palette by clicking one of the buttons, such as the **Looks** button or the **Sound** button. You can also scroll through all the blocks in the different categories in the Blocks Palette.

- **Code Area**: The Code Area (previously known as the Scripts Area in older versions of Scratch) is where you make your programs, by joining instruction blocks together. When you join blocks together, the result is called a script. The Code Area expands to fill the screen space available, so if you use a larger monitor, the Code Area will be bigger.

- **Backpack**: The Backpack at the bottom of the screen is handy for copying sprites and scripts between different projects. Click the Backpack at the bottom of the screen to open it. You can then drag sprites or scripts into it, or drag them out into your current project.

The blue stripe across the top of the screen is used for managing your projects. You can use the File menu to save your work, including downloading it to your computer. The online version of Scratch saves your updates automatically, so you won't need this often. The box containing "Untitled" is where you rename your project. Click the folder in the top right to find all your projects.

You'll see all these elements in action soon, so don't worry about memorizing the screen layout. This section is just to help you get your bearings. Remember that you can refer to the screenshot on the facing page at any time.

Use the tabs above the Blocks Palette to switch between the scripts, costumes and sounds on a sprite.

Using Scratch on tablets

You can now use Scratch on a tablet, such as an Apple iPad. Simply visit the Scratch website in your browser. You may find that Scratch runs more slowly than it does on a PC, but you should still be able to enjoy building and using many Scratch projects. If you're using a tablet, make sure you log in to the Scratch website, because you can't save projects to your device.

You can't use projects that require the keyboard, such as games that use keys to move a sprite. If the project includes **key [space] pressed?** or **when [space] key pressed** blocks (to detect any key), the project is unlikely to work well without a real keyboard. From this book, you can't play games like Super Dodgeball or Shop Cat (although they are fine to build). But you can play Spiral Rider, Space Opera, Quiz Break, Evil Robot, Photo Safari and more. I'll warn you at the start of a chapter if a project won't work on a touch-based device.

Using gestures

You'll find the touch gestures feel natural and are easy to remember. Here's how to use a touch-based device instead of a mouse:

- To "click" something, **tap** it on the screen. For example, tap to use a button or start a script.

- To "right-click" something, **tap and hold** it on the screen – for example, to duplicate a sprite in the Sprite List.

- To "hover" over a button, simply **tap** it – for example, to open the menu to add a sprite.

- You can "drag" blocks and sprites by touching them and **dragging your finger** across the screen.

- To scroll through the Blocks Palette, **swipe** it up or down.

- To move around the Code Area, **drag** its background up, down, left or right.

- To scroll in the Paint Editor (see Chapter 4), **drag the scrollbars** at the bottom and side of the canvas.

- To change the values in a block, or type something in response to an **ask** block on the Stage, **tap the box to make your virtual keyboard appear**.

With the launch of Scratch 3, touch devices are more widely supported. The previous version of Scratch was based on Flash, which didn't work on iPads. The latest version has redesigned blocks that are easier move by hand.

If you have a PC with a touchscreen, you might want to use the keyboard and touchscreen together to create your projects. Some people find it easier to use the touchscreen than the mouse.

Scrolling around the Scratch screen

If Scratch doesn't fit in your tablet's screen, you can scroll left and right by dragging the blue bar at the top. To scroll up and down, drag part of the light blue background – for example, an empty space in the Sprite List.

Using Scratch in portrait mode

If you want to see all of the Stage and the keyboard at the same time – for example, to play Quiz Break in this book – use your tablet in portrait orientation.

In the rest of this book, I'll mostly assume readers are using a keyboard and mouse, so refer back here if you need a reminder of how to use your touchscreen.

Using Scratch apps

At the time of writing, MIT is creating apps for Scratch 3. There is an unofficial app based on Scratch 1.4, called Pyonkee. It's a fun way to tinker with Scratch, but it doesn't have the cat or certain other sprites, and doesn't have newer Scratch features such as sprite cloning, extensions, and sound effect blocks.

MIT has also created ScratchJr, a reinvention of Scratch for younger children, designed for iPads and Android tablets. For tips on using ScratchJr, see our book **Cool Scratch Projects in easy steps**.

Exploring the blocks

Try experimenting with a few blocks to see what they do:

1 Click the round, blue **Motion** button to the left of the Blocks Palette to show the Motion blocks. This button is selected when you first start Scratch

2 In the Blocks Palette, click (or tap) the **move 10 steps** block. The cat on the Stage moves in the direction it's facing, to the right. Each time you click the block, the cat moves once. This block only changes the cat's position, though: you won't see its legs move

3 The number of steps is how far across the screen you want the cat to move. Click the number 10 and change it to something else. Try 50 and when you click the block, the cat moves five times as far. Whenever you see a white hole in a block, you can change what's in it

4 Rotate the cat by clicking the **turn clockwise 15 degrees** block. To change the angle of the turn, change the number. Remember to click the block to actually make the cat turn. When you click the **move 10 steps** block next time, the cat walks in its new direction

Scratch won't let the cat disappear off the screen completely. If you use numbers that are too big, the sprite will stay at the edge of the screen.

14

Above: The cat on the Stage, after I clicked "turn clockwise 15 degrees".

5 If the cat gets to the edge of the Stage, drag it back again with your mouse pointer. Click the cat, hold the mouse button down, move the cat, and then release the mouse button to drop it in place

6 Click the round, pink **Sound** button beside the Blocks Palette

7 Click the **play sound Meow until done** block. You should hear the cat make a meow sound if you have speakers on

8 Click the round, purple **Looks** button. It's beside the Blocks Palette. You can see it in the picture above

9 Click the **next costume** block to see the cat's legs move, so it appears to run on the spot. Costumes are different pictures a sprite can have, and the cat has two that show its legs in different positions (see below). In Scratch, the sprites are like the actors; they wear the costumes (different images), and they move on the Stage

All these blocks are explained later in the book, but for now it's worth spending a few minutes exploring some of the commands you can give the cat.

Scratch 3 includes new blocks to change the pitch of the sound. Try changing the numbers in the "change [pitch] effect by 10" block, clicking it, and then clicking the "play sound Meow until done" block again.

If you're using a tablet, you can tap things instead of clicking them.

Changing the backdrop

Before we make our first program, let's change the background of the Stage to something more inspiring. The background is called a backdrop in Scratch.

1 To the right of the Sprite List, there is a panel for the Stage. At the bottom, hover over the round button to open the backdrop options. Use the magnifying glass icon to choose a backdrop from the library. (You can also just click the round button to choose from the library.) The other options enable you to paint a backdrop, get a surprise backdrop, or upload a picture from your computer

2 When the library opens, click the categories at the top to view the different backdrops available, and use the scrollbar on the right to see more designs. Select the Outdoors category

3 Scroll to find, and then select, the Hill image

Creating your first program

When you click blocks in the Blocks Palette, the cat moves immediately, so this is good for testing what blocks do, but not useful for making a program. A program is a set of repeatable instructions that you can store up to carry out later. For our first Scratch program, let's make the cat walk down the hill:

1 We're going to write a program for the cat, so click the cat in the Sprite List

2 Next, check that the Code Area is open. If the middle pane shows costumes or sounds instead, click the **Code** tab above the Blocks Palette

3 Click the **Motion** button to the left of the Blocks Palette (see screenshot, right)

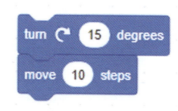

4 You make a program by dragging blocks into the Code Area from the Blocks Palette. To do this for your first block, click the **turn clockwise 15 degrees** block in the Blocks Palette, hold the mouse button down, move the mouse pointer into the Code Area and then release the mouse button. This first block will point our cat downhill, ready for its walk

5 Click the **move 10 steps** block in the Blocks Palette, drag it into the Code Area and drop it underneath the **turn clockwise 15 degrees** block. They will snap together. When blocks are joined like this they make what's known as a "script". A sprite can have more than one script, and a program might include lots of sprites with several scripts

Hot tip
If you click and drag a block that's joined to other blocks above it in the Code Area, it will break away from them, and carry all the blocks underneath it with it.

Beware
You can move blocks around the Code Area, but if you drag them into the Blocks Palette, they'll be deleted.

Don't forget
Make sure the blocks snap together, otherwise they won't work as one script. If they don't snap together, they're not close enough.

...cont'd

I wouldn't usually recommend you add the same blocks repeatedly, but we're right at the beginning of learning Scratch here. There is a more readable and elegant solution you'll discover in Chapter 2.

Hot tip

To right-click on a touchscreen device, tap and hold. When you duplicate a script, the copy is placed in the Code Area. You can drag it to the bottom of your script.

6 Click the **Control** button beside the Blocks Palette. Control blocks are used to decide when things should happen. Drag the **wait 1 seconds** block into the Code Area and snap it underneath the other two blocks. This block adds a 1-second delay. Without it, our cat would move so fast, it would appear to just jump from the start of its walk to the end. Slowing it down enables us to see what's going on. You can make it walk a bit faster by changing the delay from 1 second to 0.5 seconds

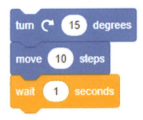

7 Right-click the **move 10 steps** block, and when the menu opens, choose **Duplicate**. This copies the block plus any blocks underneath it in your script. In our example, it copies the **move** and the **wait** blocks. Move the copy to the bottom of your program, and click to place the blocks there. You can repeat this step several times to make the cat walk further

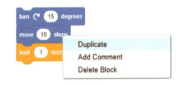

8 It's a long walk for a tiny cat, so let's make it finish its walk with a exclamation of "Phew!" in a speech bubble. Click the **Looks** button beside the Blocks Palette. Drag the **say Hello! for 2 seconds** block into the Code Area and join it to your program. Click Hello! to edit what the cat says to Phew!

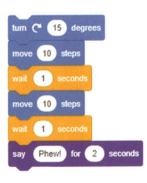

9 When you start a script's commands, it's called "running" the script. To run your script, click any of the joined-up blocks in the Code Area. Scratch carries out all the joined-up instructions in order, starting at the top and working its way down the blocks

10 What happens if you click the script to run it again? The cat turns again and walks from where it finished last time. Eventually, it'll be walking on its head. Let's add some blocks to put it in the right starting position. Click the **Motion** button beside the Blocks Palette and drag in the **point in direction 90** block and the **go to x:0 y:0** block. If the

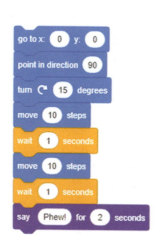

go to block has different numbers in it, edit them both to make them zero. Add these blocks to the top of your script. Can you make the cat's walk longer?

Hot tip

You can insert blocks into an existing script. Instead of dropping a block at the end of your script, drag your block over it. The blocks in the script will make room to let the new blocks in. When the blocks are in the right place, release the mouse button or your finger.

19

Hot tip

Experiment! If you use a negative number of steps in the "move 10 steps" block, the sprite moves backwards. Why not see if you can make the cat walk backwards up the hill again?

Left: A few blocks and one exhausted cat later, here's your first program.

Saving your project

A Scratch project includes all the sprites, scripts and backdrops that are used in it. It's a good idea to save your projects so you can come back to them later to reuse them or modify them.

In Scratch 3 online, your work is automatically saved for you. If your latest changes have not been saved, there will be a link to **Save Now** in the blue bar at the top of the screen, beside the folder icon that gives you access to your projects.

Your project is saved with the name Untitled plus a number. You can choose a more useful name by editing the box in the blue bar, above the Code Area, and to the right of the tabs.

In the downloadable versions of Scratch, your work isn't automatically saved for you. Use the **Save to your computer** option in the File menu to save your work.

There are additional options for saving your work in the File menu. You can find it above the Blocks Palette, as shown above. These options include:

- **Save as a copy**: This makes a copy of your project with a new name. The previously saved version of your project is left untouched. Use this if you want to experiment with your project without losing a working version of it.

- **Save to your computer**: This enables you to save your project as a file on your computer. If your internet connection fails, use this option straight away to save your work!

- **Load from your computer**: If you previously downloaded a Scratch project to your PC, or used a downloadable version of Scratch to create it, use this option to upload it to the Scratch website, so you can edit and share it there.

Opening projects

To find your projects on the Scratch 3 website, click the folder icon beside your username in the top right of the screen. You can also click your username and then click **My Stuff**.

If it says "Sign in" in place of your username, click it to sign in first.

The My Stuff section shows all your projects, with those you most recently edited nearer the top. You can see some of my projects in the screenshot below:

If you click the Share button on a project, it will be available for anyone to see, use and reuse. See Chapter 11 for more on sharing your projects.

Use the scrollbar at the right edge of your browser window to find more projects and click the **Load More** button when you get to the bottom of the list. To open a project for editing, click its **See inside** button. To simply run the project, click its screenshot.

Because projects are saved automatically, your My Stuff area quickly fills up with untitled projects. To tidy up, delete unwanted projects by clicking their **Delete** links on the right. If you delete a project by mistake, click the Trash folder on the left, and then click the **Put back** button to recover the project. You can't delete a shared project without unsharing it first (see page 209 in Chapter 11).

In downloaded versions of Scratch, you open projects by clicking to open the File menu at the top of the screen and then choosing Open.

Opening shared projects

You can open the projects that other people have shared on the Scratch website too. Visit the website at **https://scratch.mit.edu** and click **Explore** at the top of the screen.

Use the buttons to choose a category of projects to explore. The triangle to the right of the project categories opens a menu that you can use to find projects that are trending, popular, or recent.

Hot tip

If you are logged in, you can click the Remix button to create your own version of a project shared on the Scratch website. All the projects on the Scratch website are shared on the understanding that others can learn from them, and create adaptations of them. You can find a Remix button on the project's page, and another in the blue bar at the top of the screen when you look inside the project.

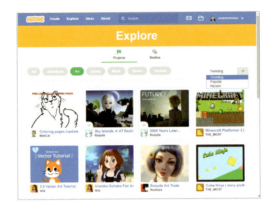

Click a project to go to its page. The instructions on the right tell you how to use the project, and you click the **green flag** button to run it, either the one in the middle of the project or the one above the project's display. If you like what you see, and you want to know how it was done, click the **See inside** button in the top right to go into the editor and see the code.

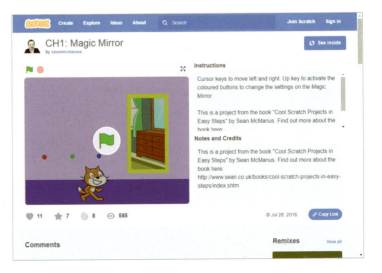

2 Drawing with Scratch

Find your bearings on the Scratch Stage, learn how to move sprites and draw with them, and discover how loops make it easy to repeat parts of your program. You'll also make an interactive art program called Rainbow Painter.

You can click and drag your sprites around the Stage to reposition them while you're writing your programs. It's a good idea to use the "go to x:0 y:0" block to position them in the program, though, otherwise they might start off somewhere unexpected. If your sprite moves in the program, it won't be in the same position the second time the program is used. Other people can experiment with your program too, and might move sprites around before it starts.

Understanding coordinates

You can use the sprites in Scratch to draw on the Stage. It's a great way to familiarize yourself with how to move sprites, and the technique can be used to create designs that your sprites can interact with, as you'll see when we make a game in Chapter 3.

First, let's take a look at how you position sprites on the Stage. Each position on the Stage has a grid reference, similar to those used on maps. The position across the Stage horizontally is called x, and the position up or down the Stage is called y.

When you start a new project, the cat is in the middle of the Stage, and this position has the grid reference x=0 and y=0.

Here's a map of the grid references on the Stage, after I've moved the cat to the bottom-left quarter of the Stage:

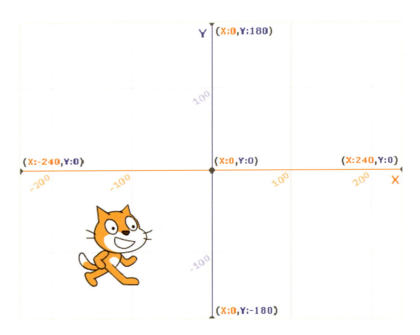

As you can see, the numbers for the y coordinate run from -180 at the bottom of the Stage, up to +180 at the top of the Stage.

The numbers for the x coordinate run from -240 at the left edge of the Stage, up to +240 at the right edge of the Stage.

An easy way to remember which way around x and y should be is that "x is a cross" (and "across").

1 Click the **Motion** button beside the Blocks Palette

Don't forget

To start a new project, click the File menu and then click New. If the File menu isn't showing, click Create in the blue menu at the top of the screen.

2 To place a sprite at a particular position on screen, use the **go to x:0 y:0** block. This block is most often used to place a sprite in its starting position. Click it and drag it into the Code Area

3 The numbers in the block return a sprite to the middle of the screen, but you can change the coordinates. Click the white space beside x: and enter -120. Click the white space beside y: (or press the Tab key) and type -90

Hot tip

You can change the numbers in the "go to x:0 y:0" block in the Blocks Palette, and Scratch sometimes changes them, too. If you're often reusing the same coordinates, that might save you time, because you can then drag the same coordinates in with your block. In this book, I'll assume this block is set to x:0 y:0 in the Blocks Palette. You can easily change the values in it, so it doesn't matter if you see something different on your screen.

4 Click the block to see the cat go to its new position, in the bottom-left quarter of the screen

5 Try changing the numbers in the block and clicking it to see where the cat moves around the Stage

Scratch 3 adds a new glide block. Use it to glide to a random position, or the mouse-pointer.

If you change the x or y position by too much, you'll break the illusion of animation. It looks better if you use lots of small movements, rather than one big one.

In your program, any blocks joined underneath the "glide" block won't start until after the glide has finished. Using time values of more than a second can slow down your program a lot.

Changing a sprite's position

There are several blocks you can use to change a sprite's position using coordinates. To find them, click the **Motion** button beside the Blocks Palette:

- **glide 1 secs to x:0 y:0**: This block makes your sprite glide across the screen to its new position.

It travels in a straight line. You can change the x and y coordinates in the block, and change how long the movement takes from 1 second to a value like 0.5 or 0.25 (for a faster glide), or to a bigger number for a slower one.

- **change x by 10**: This block makes your sprite move 10 positions to the right on the Stage. It doesn't affect its y position, and works independently of which way the sprite is facing. To increase how far the sprite moves, use a bigger number.

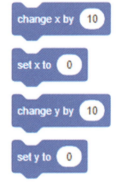

- **change x by -10**: To make your sprite move left, change the value in the **change x by** block to a negative number. To make the sprite move further, use a bigger negative number.

- **change y by 10**: This block makes your sprite move 10 positions up the Stage. It doesn't affect its horizontal position, and also works independently of which way the sprite is facing. Change the 10 to a bigger number for a bigger movement.

- **change y by -10**: Similar to the way you make a sprite move left, you can make a sprite move down the screen by changing the 10 in the **change y by** block to a negative number. For a bigger movement, use a bigger negative number.

- **set x to 0**: This block changes your sprite's horizontal position to a specific number without affecting its vertical position.

- **set y to 0**: This block changes your sprite's vertical position to a specific number without affecting its horizontal position.

Using the pen

The pen in Scratch enables a sprite to draw a line as it moves around the Stage.

Before you can use the Pen blocks, you need to add them to your Blocks Palette. Click the **Add Extension** button at the bottom of the Blocks Palette (shown above), and then choose to add the Pen blocks.

You'll see the Pen blocks are added to the Blocks Palette, with a button to show them on the left too. The new blocks are:

- **erase all**: This clears all the drawing on the Stage, but doesn't disturb the backdrop or any sprites.

- **stamp**: This block prints a copy of the sprite on the Stage, so when the sprite moves on, it will leave a picture of itself behind. It's just a picture of the sprite, not a copy of the sprite that you can control. In Chapter 4, you'll learn how to clone and duplicate sprites, so you can control the copies.

- **pen down**: This is like putting the pen down on a piece of paper. After you use this, your sprite leaves a line wherever it goes.

- **pen up**: This block stops your sprite from drawing as it moves. Sprites start with the pen up, so they won't leave a line unless you put the pen down. If you have been using the pen, remember to lift the pen up before moving a sprite if you don't want it to leave a line behind it. For example, you might want to use this block before moving a sprite to its starting position in a project, in case the pen is still down from the last time the project ran.

When you come to add multiple sprites in your projects later, each sprite will have its own pen and its own settings for the pen color and size, and for whether the pen is up or down.

You can stamp a sprite on the Stage even when that sprite is hidden.

If you're using the pen in your program, it's a good idea to start with the "erase all" block so you always start with a clean Stage.

...cont'd

Hot tip

Click the numbers in the blocks and you can edit them to different numbers.

NEW

When you see a symbol on a block (like the pen shown in these blocks), it means the blocks require an extension. You'll need to add it to the Blocks Palette before you can use those blocks.

Below: The pen colors from 0 to 200.

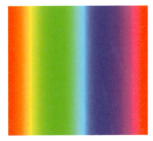

- **set pen color to [color]**: Click the color in this block to choose which color you'd like to use with the pen, and its saturation (or intensity) and brightness. To get black, use the lowest brightness value. For white, use the maximum brightness and lowest saturation. You can also use the pipette to pick a color from the Stage.

Pipette

- **change pen color by 10**: Each color has a number, and the colors are arranged like a rainbow, going through shades of red, orange, yellow, green, blue and pink. Use this block to change the pen color to a higher number. Using a negative number will change the pen color to a lower number. You can use the menu in this block to choose to change the saturation, brightness or transparency instead of the color.

- **set pen color to 50**: You can also set the color to a specific number, between 0 and 200. If you use higher numbers, they do work, but the same colors repeat. Color 350 is the same as 150, for example. At the bottom left of the page you can see the pen colors from 0 on the left to 200 on the right. By clicking the word **color** in this block, or in the **change pen color** block, you can open a menu. Use it to choose to change the saturation, brightness or transparency of the pen instead of its color.

- **change pen size by 1**: This block increases the pen size. Use a negative number to decrease it.

- **set pen size to 1**: Use this block to set the pen size to a specific width. Anything larger than 5 leaves a thick line.

Drawing a house in Scratch

You can use what you've learned about moving sprites and the pen to draw pictures on the Stage. Follow these steps to draw a house:

1 Change the backdrop to xy-grid, which puts a grid onto the Stage to help you work out coordinates. You can type "xy" into the search box at the top of the Choose a Backdrop screen to find it

2 Use the **Add Extension** button to add the Pen blocks. Click the Cat sprite, and click the **Code** tab to get ready

3 There's a potential pitfall here: if the pen is down, then the sprite will draw a line you don't want as it moves into place. To fix that, lift the pen before moving the sprite. Click the **Pen** button beside the Blocks Palette and drag the **erase all** block and the **pen up** block into the Code Area

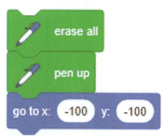

4 Click the **Motion** button and drag in the **go to x:0 y:0** block. Change the numbers in it to x:-100 y:-100, so it puts the sprite in the correct starting position

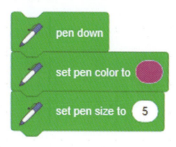

5 Next, we should get ready to draw. Use **pen down** to start drawing, and set the pen color and size to something that will stand out from the grid pattern. Add these blocks to the bottom of your script

Hot tip

The picture is drawn almost instantly. To slow it down so you can see what's happening, add some "wait" blocks between the movement blocks. You can find the "wait" block among the Control blocks.

29

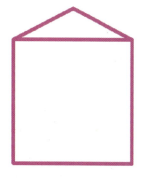

Above: The house we're drawing.

...cont'd

Hot tip

Why not see if you can add windows and a door? Remember to lift the pen before repositioning the pen inside the square.

6 Our sprite is now positioned in the bottom-left corner of our house. To draw the square, move the sprite up (increasing the y coordinate), right (increasing the x coordinate), down (decreasing the y coordinate), and left (decreasing the x coordinate). Each line has a length of 200, so the sprite ends where it started. Click the **Motion** button and add these blocks to your script

7 To draw the roof, we need to move the cat to the top-left corner of the house first. To draw a straight diagonal line, we use the **go to x:0 y:0 block** to move to the tip of the roof, and use it again to move to the right corner of the house. Drag in these blocks and add them to the end of your script

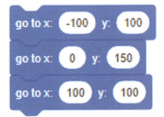

8 Click your script to run it, and you should see the scene below on the Stage

Above: The finished program.

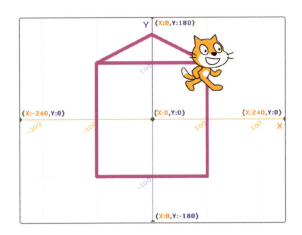

Using directions to move

As you saw last chapter, there is another way you can move sprites in Scratch, which is to point them in a particular direction and then move them forwards in that direction.

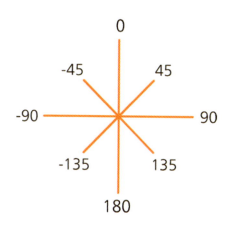

The direction numbers go from -179 to 180. Up is direction 0, down is 180, left is -90 and right is 90. See the compass diagram on the right.

Here are the blocks you use to move using directions:

- **move 10 steps**: This moves your sprite forwards. In the case of the cat, this usually means the direction it's facing. You can change the number of steps, and a negative number makes the sprite go backwards.

- **turn clockwise 15 degrees**: This rotates your sprite clockwise by 15 degrees. You can change the number of degrees. You can use a negative number to turn the other way, but you will rarely need to, because of the next block.

- **turn counter-clockwise 15 degrees**: This block turns your sprite in the other direction.

- **point towards**: This block is used to point a sprite towards another sprite, or the mouse pointer.

- **point in direction 90**: This makes your sprite point in a particular direction. There is a dial control you can use to choose a direction (see right). You can also type in a number of your choice, such as 90 for right, or 0 for up.

Don't forget

Which is better? Moving using coordinates, or using directions? There's no right answer to that: it depends on your project. Part of the art of Scratch is to choose the best approach for each project you write. We'll use both methods in this book, sometimes in the same program.

Hot tip

When you turn your sprite, Scratch makes sure the numbers make sense automatically. For example, when the direction is 180 (down) and you rotate clockwise by 90 degrees, Scratch turns the resulting direction into -90 (left) instead of 270, which would be mathematically correct, but is outside the range of directions Scratch uses.

Keeping sprites upright

One of the problems with rotating sprites is that it can look strange, even in the context of a game. When you rotate the cat to move up (direction 0), it looks like it's climbing the walls:

You can rotate your sprite without using blocks if you need a quick fix. Use the direction box in the panel above the Sprite List. Drag the dial in a circle to rotate the sprite. There are also options to set the rotation style here, to all around, left-right, or don't rotate.

Worse still, when its direction is set to left (-90), the cat looks like it's walking on its head.

To avoid this problem, you can change the rotation style of the sprite. There are three styles to choose from:

- **all around**: This is the "normal" setting that makes the sprite turn all the way around depending on its direction, and can make the sprite appear to defy logic and gravity. The sprite turns to face the direction it will move in.

- **left-right**: This keeps your sprite's feet on the ground and makes it face either left or right, but never up or down or at an angle. You can move the sprite in any direction, but it will always face right or left.

- **don't rotate**: This stops the sprite from visibly changing when its direction changes. You can still change its direction and move it in that direction, but the sprite will always look exactly the same. The Cat sprite, for example, will always face right, even when it's moving left.

Setting rotation style using a block

The block **set rotation style** can be used to change the rotation style. Click the **Motion** button and scroll to find this block near the end of the Motion blocks. You can scroll using the scrollbar (on the right edge of the Blocks Palette) or mouse scrollwheel, or you can swipe on a tablet.

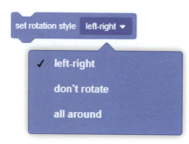

You can click the menu in the block to choose which of the rotation styles you'd like to use. To set the rotation style, click the block in the Blocks Palette, or, better still, build it into your script.

Testing different rotation styles

To see the effect of using different rotation styles, use this short script. Set the rotation style in the first block, and then click the script to run it. Click the red Stop button above the Stage to stop the script, then set a different rotation style and run the script again.

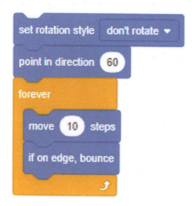

In Scratch 3, you can scroll through all the blocks in the Blocks Palette, making it much easier to find the one you need.

Although you can change the rotation style using the information panel, it's better to do it using a block in your program, just in case someone has changed the rotation style before using the program.

The right way up for a sprite in Scratch is facing right. That means you should always draw your own sprites facing right (see Chapter 4).

33

Drawing using directions

Earlier in this chapter, you saw how to draw a house by moving the cat to specific points on the Stage.

You can also use directions to achieve the same effect.

This page shows a script that draws a square. You can save time when building it by duplicating the blocks to move and turn: right-click the **move 200 steps** block and choose Duplicate in the menu that opens.

Here's how it works:

- The first six blocks are the same as we used when drawing the house, and just prepare our sprite for drawing.

- The next block turns it to point up the screen.

- Then we move it forwards 200 steps, which draws a line up the screen.

- We rotate 90 degrees right (so the sprite is facing right), move it again to draw the top of the square.

- Then we turn and draw a line down, and turn to draw a line to the left.

There's a lot of repetition in there: we have included the same two instructions four times in a row.

It works, but it's laborious to create and hard to read. Luckily, there is a better solution.

Below: This is what the result looks like.

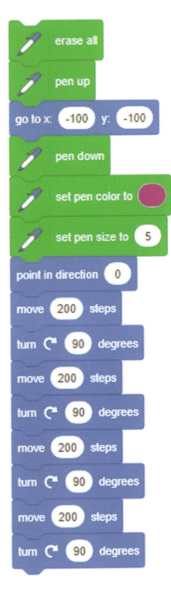

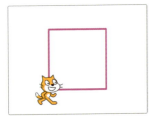

Making shapes using repeat

In our square drawing program, it would be far simpler to tell the program to go forward and turn right four times than it is to list out every turn and movement.

The **repeat 10** block makes this possible. It is one of the Control blocks, which determine whether and how often things happen in a program. It's shaped like a bracket, and you put the blocks you want to repeat inside it. You change the number in the block's frame to say how often you want it to repeat the blocks inside.

Here is how you can use the **repeat 10** block to draw a square:

The blocks to move and turn sit inside the **repeat** block's bracket, and the **repeat** block repeats them four times. Repeating sections of a script are often called loops. It's easier to see what's happening in this program than it was when we had so many drawing instructions, and it's easier to modify the program too.

What if you want a hexagon? You can just increase the number of times the sprite moves and turns, from 4 to 6 (for the 6 sides and angles), and also change the size of the turn to 60 degrees. I also made the hexagon smaller, so it fits on the Stage. The number of steps the sprite moves decides how long each side is.

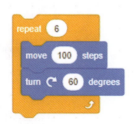

You can modify this loop to draw any shape with sides of the same length. To work out the angle of the turn, divide 360 by the number of sides. To alter the size of the shape, change the distance the sprite moves for each line.

For best results, add these example loops after the first six blocks from the previous example that set up the Stage.

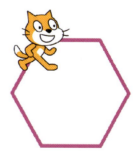

Above: The square becomes a hexagon.

Take care with where you put your blocks. For example, if you put the block to change the pen color inside the inner "repeat" block that draws the hexagon, the pen color will change with each line. That doesn't matter so much with abstract demonstrations like this, but it can cause huge problems in more elaborate programs.

Hot tip

A loop inside a loop is called a nested loop.

Hot tip

The outer loop repeats 72 times because it turns 5 degrees each time. 72 times 5 degrees makes 360 degrees, a full circle.

Putting loops inside loops

You can put **repeat** blocks inside each other. Start a new project and try making this program. It creates a pattern of overlapping hexagons as shown below.

The first few blocks position the sprite, erase previous drawings, and set the pen up.

After that, we have the first of our loops, which will repeat 72 times. If you look inside it, you can see the first thing it does is use another loop that repeats 6 times to draw a hexagon.

After that loop has finished and the hexagon is drawn, the pen color is changed and the sprite is turned by 5 degrees. Then the process repeats, with another hexagon drawn, the color changed and the sprite rotated until 72 hexagons are on screen.

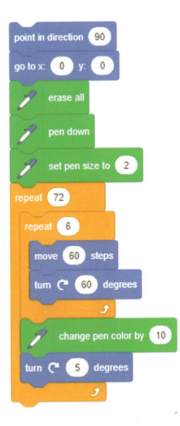

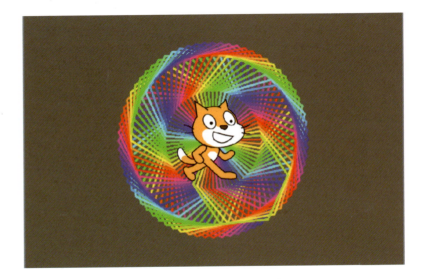

Creating Rainbow Painter

To close this chapter, here's a simple art program called Rainbow Painter that enables you to paint with a striped pen across the starry night sky. It shows you how simple it can be to make a program that interacts with the user. Once you've written it, you can use this program to make your own digital designs:

1 Start a new project, and change the backdrop to stars. It's in the Space category

2 Click the cat in the Sprite List and click the **Code** tab to open the Code Area

3 It's possible to hide a sprite, so it's not shown on the screen but it can still move around and draw on the Stage. We'll use a hidden sprite that follows the mouse pointer, or your finger on a tablet. This sprite will draw on the Stage. Click the **Looks** button beside the Blocks Palette to find the **hide** block and drag it into the Code Area

The color and design of the blocks provides a hint about where you can find them in the Blocks Palette. To find the blocks with a pen on them, click the pen icon beside the Blocks Palette. To find the purple blocks, click the purple Looks button.

Don't forget

37

4 Add the Pen extension and then drag in the drawing blocks shown above to set up the program

5 As well as the **repeat** block, there is a **forever** block that repeats whatever is inside it endlessly. Find it in the **Control** section of the Blocks Palette

Hot tip

Notice that there's no slot on the bottom of the "forever" block for other blocks to lock into. That's because a forever loop never ends, so any blocks underneath it would never be used.

6 Drag the block in and join it to your script

...cont'd

Hot tip

You can stop a program that runs forever, or any other program, by clicking the red hexagonal Stop button above the Stage.

7 Drag in the Motion block **go to [random position]** and click the menu in it to choose mouse-pointer. This block moves your invisible sprite to the mouse pointer or your finger on a touchscreen. As you move the mouse or your finger, the sprite follows you and draws a line behind it. Put this block inside the bracket of your **forever** block

8 Drag in the block to change the pen color by 10, so the color is continuously changing. This block, too, goes inside the bracket of the forever block

When you run the program and move your mouse pointer or finger over the Stage, you'll leave a rainbow-colored line. Here's a picture of me wearing sunglasses, drawn using Rainbow Painter. Experiment with changing the pen size for bolder lines.

Above: The final program looks like this.

3 Spiral Rider

Learn how to make your first game, including using the green flag to start scripts, using variables to store a number, moving a sprite with the keyboard or touchscreen, and letting Scratch make simple decisions about which blocks should run.

Introducing Spiral Rider

Poor Freddy Fish has bought a new T-shirt and the tag in the back is really itching. Chris the Crab has claws that could clip the tag off, if only the pair could meet up. Chris has crawled through a maze of passages in the rock. Can you help Freddy get there?

Behind this silly premise lies a game that will use what you have already learned about Scratch and take it further to help you make your first real game. You'll learn how to:

- Keep track of a number, so you can make a square spiral with ever decreasing line lengths.

- Use multiple sprites, and use the green flag to synchronize them.

- Move sprites with the keyboard or using a touch control on a tablet device.

- Make a sprite move automatically.

- Detect when a sprite hits something.

In this game, you control the fish using the arrow keys or by tapping it to make it turn. You must turn at the right time on each corner to navigate the spiral successfully.

Hot tip

If you can't get the examples to work, or if you want to take a shortcut, you can find them online. Visit the author's profile on the Scratch website at **https://scratch.mit.edu/ users/seanmcmanus/** or follow the link at **https://www.sean. co.uk/scratch/** or at **www.ineasysteps.com/ resources/download**

Hot tip

You can play this game on a tablet. We'll add a special touch control so you can turn by tapping the fish.

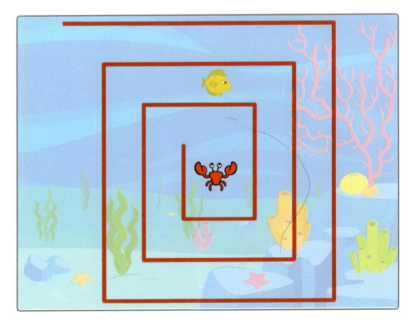

Using the green flag

So far we've started our programs by just clicking the stack of blocks we want to run. There are a few problems with this:

- When someone else uses the program, they might not know which stack of blocks they should run first.

- It's not user-friendly. Someone who wants to just play your game should be able to do so without having to look at its blocks.

- It's difficult to synchronize different sprites to start at the same time.

Scratch provides a simple solution to problems like this with the green flag, a button above the Stage used to start programs. Scripts on different sprites can detect when that button is clicked, and can then start at the same time.

People using Scratch programs know how to start programs using the green flag too. When you share programs through the Scratch website, they're shown with a prominent green flag button in the middle of the Stage, like a play button on a video.

There is a block you can use at the top of your stack of blocks to start them when the green flag is clicked:

It has a curved top because no other blocks can connect to the top of it: it is always the first block in its stack. Blocks shaped like this are called hat blocks.

This block is an Events block. Events blocks are used for detecting when things happen, such as buttons being clicked. To find the Events blocks, either scroll through the Blocks Palette, or click the yellow Events button beside the Blocks Palette.

Hot tip

You can still click a stack of blocks to run them, even if there is a "when green flag clicked" block at the top of it. This can be useful for testing scripts.

Above: When you share a program on the Scratch website, it has a big green flag button so users know how to start it.

42

Creating variables

We're going to draw our spiral starting at the outside and working our way inwards. The way we draw a spiral is similar to how we draw a square: we draw a line, turn 90 degrees and repeat until we reach the middle. The big difference is that the lines get shorter as we move towards the middle.

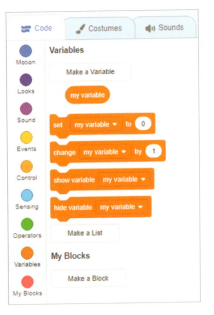

That means we need a way to remember the length of the line, and to shorten it. Variables are used in Scratch (and other programming languages) to store information we want to remember, so we can reuse it and change it. You could use a variable to keep track of a score, the number of lives left, the player's name, or the right answer in a word guessing game.

Start a new project, and click on the Cat sprite, which we will use to draw our spiral. Let's make a variable to store the length of the lines in the spiral:

1 Click the round, orange **Variables** button beside the Blocks Palette. It's selected in the picture above

2 Click the **Make a Variable** button in the Blocks Palette, also shown above

3 A pop-up box appears, like the one shown on the right

4 The first thing we need to do is name our variable. You can use spaces in Scratch variable names. Type **line length** into the box, but don't press Enter yet

5 When you make a variable, you can choose whether it can be used by all sprites or just the current sprite. You can't change this later, so pause for thought here. For simplicity, we'll make this variable for all sprites, although only this sprite will use it. (If we wanted to use this same variable name on other sprites too, we'd need to create this variable to be used by just this sprite)

6 You can make a cloud variable. This means the variable is shared between everyone using your program on the Scratch website. They could, for example, share the high score. Leave the Cloud variable box unchecked (unticked)

7 Click the **OK** button

8 The Blocks Palette contains blocks for managing your variable. The block with rounded ends has a checkbox beside it. When checked, it shows your variable and its value on the Stage. We don't need that now, so uncheck it. The blocks to set and change the variable values have menus in them that you can use to choose which variable you'd like to change, and a box where you can type a number or some text

Hot tip

If a variable is set up for just one sprite, other sprites can't use its value or change its value. That stops them causing errors by interfering with a variable they shouldn't, so it's often considered a good idea.

Beware

Cloud variables can only be used for numbers and are not available to new Scratchers.

Hot tip

Two sprites can have variables with the same name that work completely independently. This happens, for example, if you give a sprite a variable for that sprite only, and then duplicate that sprite. See duplication in Chapter 4.

43

Drawing a spiral

We'll use our new variable to draw a spiral on the Stage. Follow these steps to add the blocks needed to your Cat sprite:

1 Click the **Events** button. Drag the **when green flag clicked** block into the Code Area to start your script

2 It looks best if our spiral seems to magically appear from nowhere, so let's make the cat invisible. Click the **Looks** button beside the Blocks Palette and add the **hide** block to your stack

3 To put our cat in its starting position (the top left of the Stage), click the **Motion** button beside the Blocks Palette and drag the **go to x:0 y:0** and **point in direction 90** blocks into your stack. Change the values in the **go to** block to x: -180 and y: 170 by clicking and editing the numbers

4 Click the **Add Extension** button in the bottom-left corner. Add the Pen extension

5 Click **Pen** beside the Blocks Palette, and drag in these blocks. Join them to your script so far. These blocks clear the screen of any drawing that's already there, and get the pen ready to draw this time

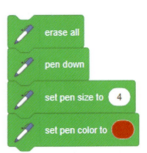

6 We need to set the starting value of our *line length* variable. I've chosen 340, because the height of the Stage is 360, so a maximum spiral height of 340 fits comfortably. Click the **Variables** button. Drag the block **set line length to 0** into your script. Then click the box in the block and change the 0 to 340

Hot tip

The "go to x:0 y:0" block might have different numbers in it in the Blocks Palette. That's okay, because you can always change them.

44

7 Our spiral uses two loops, one inside the other. The inner loop draws a line, turns 90 degrees and then does the same again, so it repeats its blocks twice in total. The line length is then shortened, and the process repeats, six times in total. In the picture below, I've changed the pen color each time the line length is shortened. Lines of the same color are drawn by the same inner loop

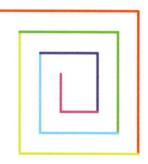

Hot tip

You can see the complete program for drawing a spiral on page 46.

8 Click the **Control** button beside the Blocks Palette and drag the **repeat 10** block into your stack. Drag another **repeat 10** block in, and set the outer loop to repeat six times, and the inner loop to repeat twice. Join these to the end of your script so far

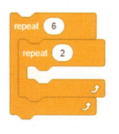

9 Click the **Motion** button beside the Blocks Palette, and drag in **move 10 steps** and **turn clockwise 15 degrees**. Change the number in the **turn** block to 90 degrees. These blocks go inside your **repeat 2** bracket

...cont'd

10 You can use a variable in place of a number. Instead of moving 10 steps, or any other fixed number, we want to move the same number as we've stored in our *line length* variable. To do this, we replace the number in the **move** block with the variable name. Click the **Variables** button beside the Blocks Palette, and drag the rounded block containing the *line length* variable name into the **move 10 steps** block

11 After the inner loop ends, and an L shape has been drawn, we want to shorten the length of the lines. Drag in the Variables block **change line length by 1**. Make sure it joins underneath the inner **repeat** block, and doesn't go inside its bracket. Change the number in it to -50

12 You can see our finished script to the right. Click the **green flag** button above the Stage to see your spiral appear!

Changing the backdrop

We have our spiral, but we can make our game look much more interesting by adding in an underwater backdrop:

1 Add one of the underwater backdrops to your project. There are two to choose from in the Underwater category. I've chosen the one that looks like scenery from a cartoon

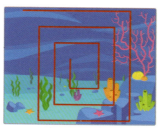

Hot tip

The ghost graphic effect uses a number from 0 to 100, which is a percentage. When the ghost effect on the backdrop is at 100%, the backdrop is invisible.

2 The backdrop is quite vibrant, and makes it hard to see what's going on in the game. We can tone it down using a graphic effect. To do that, we will add some blocks to the Stage. Click the Stage icon beside the Sprite List. It looks like your chosen backdrop. Open the Code Area by clicking the **Code** tab above the Blocks Palette

3 Click the **Events** button beside the Blocks Palette. Drag the **when green flag clicked** block into the Code Area

4 Click the **Looks** button beside the Blocks Palette. Drag in the block **set color effect to 0** and join it to **when green flag clicked**

5 In the **set effect** block, click the menu to choose the ghost effect. Change the number in the block to 60. This will fade the backdrop out by 60% when the green flag is clicked, making it easier to see the spiral we've drawn and the sprites we'll add to the Stage shortly

Hot tip

You can also apply the graphic effects to sprites, as you'll see later on. The ghost effect makes sprites transparent.

6 When you click the green flag, the backdrop lightens (see right)

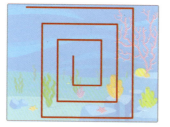

Adding sprites

Our game will use three sprites: the invisible Cat sprite, which draws the spiral; Freddy the Fish; and Chris the Crab.

1 At the bottom of the Sprite List is a button for adding a new sprite. When you hover over it, a menu opens. You can choose a sprite from the library, paint a new sprite (see Chapter 4), get a random (or surprise) sprite, or upload a picture you've already made.

Choose to get a sprite from the library. If you're using a mouse you can also just click the round button to go straight to this option next time

2 The sprite library opens, and looks similar to the library of backdrops you used previously. You can click categories at the top to browse the different sprites available. Click the Animals category, then click the crab to add it to your project

3 Repeat the process, but this time select the sprite Fish, which is also in the Animals category. Use the scrollbar on the right of the sprite library to see more sprites

Animating the crab

When the game starts, we need to position the crab in the middle of the spiral and set its size. To make it look more lifelike, we can make it bob from side to side during the game. Follow these steps to create the script for the crab:

1 Click the crab in the Sprite List to make sure you're adding your script to the right sprite

Sprite	Crab		x	12	y	-30	Stage

Size 40 Direction 90

Sprite1 Crab Fish

Backdrops 3

2 Click the **Events** button beside the Blocks Palette. Drag the **when green flag clicked** block into the Code Area

3 Click the **Motion** button beside the Blocks Palette and drag the **go to x:0 y:0** block into your script

4 Change the values in the **go to** block to x: 10 and y: -30 by clicking and editing the numbers

5 Click the **Looks** button beside the Blocks Palette and drag in the **set size to 100%** block. Click the number in the block and change it to 40. I found the right size by trying different numbers. I wanted the crab to be as big as possible, but still fit in the middle of the spiral

6 Check your script so far (right)

when ⚑ clicked

go to x: 10 y: -30

set size to 40 %

Hot tip

You could position the crab by just dragging it onto the Stage, but it's better to make sure everything is in its right place every time your program runs.

Beware

When you have more than one sprite in a program take care to make sure you're adding your scripts to the right sprite.

...cont'd

 Click the **Control** button beside the Blocks Palette and drag the **forever** block into your script. We'll use this to make our crab hop left and right all the time the game is playing

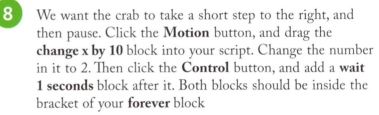

 We want the crab to take a short step to the right, and then pause. Click the **Motion** button, and drag the **change x by 10** block into your script. Change the number in it to 2. Then click the **Control** button, and add a **wait 1 seconds** block after it. Both blocks should be inside the bracket of your **forever** block

9 If we click the green flag now (try it!), the crab will slowly walk away. We want it to just hop left and right. In the bracket of the **forever** block, add another **change x by 10** block and another **wait 1 seconds** block. Change the number in the movement block from 10 to -2

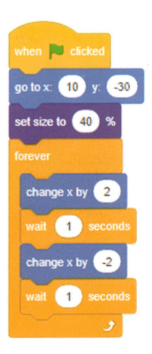

 Test it works by clicking the green flag above the Stage. You can click and drag the fish on the Stage out of the way

Enabling keyboard control

There are a couple of different techniques you can use to make a sprite move in a game, as you'll see in other projects in this book. For this game, we'll make the fish swim all the time, so players have to steer it to stop it hitting the spiral. When the player presses one of the arrow keys, we'll change Freddy's direction. There is a block you can use to start a script when a particular key is pressed on the keyboard. (We'll add touch controls shortly too.)

 1 Click the fish in the Sprite List to make sure you're adding your script to the right sprite

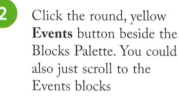

Events blocks have changed color in Scratch 3. In the previous version of Scratch, they were brown.

2 Click the round, yellow **Events** button beside the Blocks Palette. You could also just scroll to the Events blocks

3 Drag the **when [space] key pressed** block into the Code Area. Like the **when green flag clicked** block, this is a hat block and has a curved top because nothing can go above it. This block always starts off the stack of blocks it is connected to

...cont'd

4 Click the menu in this block, and you can choose which key you want to detect. Select **up arrow**

5 Click the **Motion** button beside the Blocks Palette. Drag in the **point in direction 90** block, and join it to your **when up arrow key pressed** block. Click the direction menu to open it and then click **(0) up**

52

Hot tip

6 Repeat these steps to detect the down, left and right arrow keys, and to change the direction of the fish when they're pressed. It's okay to have several different and unconnected scripts for a sprite. Here's what the finished movement key detection scripts should look like

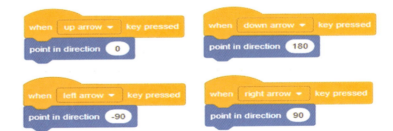

7 Press the arrow keys to check the fish changes direction. Note that it won't actually move around the screen yet

Enabling touch control

If you're using Scratch on a device that doesn't have a keyboard, you can add a control to this project so you can play with a touchscreen.

When you play using a keyboard, you press a key for the direction you want the fish to travel in, which requires four keys. For touch controls, I've opted for something simpler: when you tap the fish, it turns right. This works in this game because you'll only ever turn right to go around a corner of the spiral.

1 Click the fish in the Sprite List to make sure you're adding your script to the right sprite

2 Click the round, yellow **Events** button beside the Blocks Palette, or scroll to the Events blocks

3 Drag the **when this sprite clicked** block into the Code Area. Like the **when green flag clicked** block, this is a hat block that starts off the script underneath it, in this case when the sprite is clicked or tapped

4 Click the **Motion** button beside the Blocks Palette. Drag in the **turn 15 degrees** block, and join it to your **when this sprite clicked** block

5 Change the number in the turn block from 15 to 90. Your finished script should look like the one on the right

6 Test it! Tap the fish to see it rotate, or try clicking it with your mouse if you don't have a touchscreen

The optimum size of the fish was discovered by experimentation. I played the game a few times to work out a size that fitted in the spiral, but was still big enough to make it a challenge to dodge the walls.

Don't forget

The color of the blocks usually gives you a clue where to find them in the Blocks Palette. To find the purple blocks, for example, click the purple Looks button. To find the blocks with a pen picture in, click the Pen button.

Making the fish move

Our script for the fish puts it in the starting position (the bottom left of the screen), points it in the right direction (up), and adjusts its size so it can fit in the spiral. The script then keeps it moving until it hits either the spiral or the crab. If it hits the spiral, we display a message that says "Ouch". Otherwise, we display a happy message because the player has reached the crab.

Here's how you make the script for the fish:

 1 Click the fish in the Sprite List to make sure you're adding your scripts to the right sprite

2 The first few blocks will be familiar to you by now, so drag them into the Code Area and change the values in them. The fish should start at x:-180 y:-140, pointing in direction 0 (up), and with a size of 40%. I've used a **switch costume** block to choose a different picture of the fish. Each sprite can have multiple images, known as costumes. The image for fish-d is easier to tap on touchscreen devices, and has a shorter tail. Fish with longer tails are more likely to hit the spiral with them when they turn a corner, making the game much harder

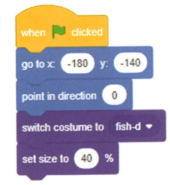

3 To keep the fish moving until it hits something, you use the **repeat until** block. It's a Control block. Drag it in and join it to your script

4 Inside the bracket of the **repeat until** block, add a **move 10 steps** block, and change the number in it to 4. This is all you need inside the **repeat until** bracket. Remember you've added four other scripts to change the fish's direction when a key is pressed

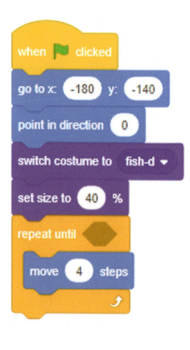

To speed the game up, change the number 4 in the "move 4 steps" block to a higher number.

5 The **repeat until** block has a diamond-shaped hole in it. This is where you tell Scratch that you want it to repeat the loop until the fish hits the spiral or the crab. Click the **Operators** button beside the Blocks Palette, and drag the **or** block into the diamond hole

Hot tip

The "or" Operator block is used because we want to move the fish until it hits the crab *or* the spiral. There is another Operator block you can use to check whether two things are both true. If we had used the "and" block instead of the "or" block, the fish would move until it was touching both the spiral and the crab.

55

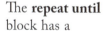

...cont'd

Glance at the Sprite List if you're not sure which sprite is which: you can see the sprite's picture and name there.

Beware

If you select a red color at the edge of the line that makes up the spiral, the game might not work correctly. Scratch softens the lines it draws by using a lighter color at the edges. You need to pick the solid red from the middle of the spiral's line for your script to correctly detect that color when the fish hits it. My screenshot on the right shows how to do this: make sure you go fully inside the line when picking the color with the pipette.

6 To see whether the fish has hit the spiral or the crab, you use two Sensing blocks. Click the **Sensing** button beside the Blocks Palette. Drag the **touching mouse-pointer?** block and drop it onto the left of the green **or** block. The

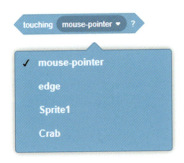

touching? block is used for checking whether a sprite is touching another sprite, the mouse pointer, or the edge of the Stage. Use the menu in it to select Crab

7 Drag the **touching color?** block into the other side of the **or** block. Click the square of color inside your **touching color?** block, and then click the pipette at the bottom of the color menu that opens. Move the magnifier over the Stage (using your mouse, or by dragging your finger on a touchscreen). Click your mouse button or release your finger when the red in the middle of the spiral is selected. Don't pick a red at the edge of the line (see Beware tip)

8 Click the **green flag** button above the Stage. You should be able to move the fish until it hits the spiral or the crab

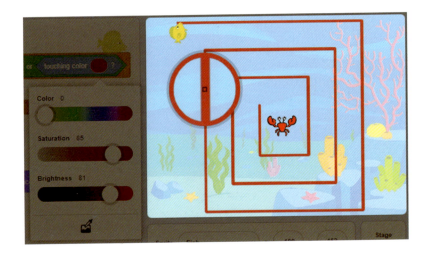

Adding Game Over messages

There are two ways the game can end: the fish is touching the crab (which means the player won), or the fish is touching the color of the spiral, which means they crashed. We can use an **if... then... else** block to display a different message, depending on how the game ended:

 1
The **if... then... else** block is a Control block. Drag it into the Code Area and join it to the bottom of your script

The game is surprisingly tricky. It looks simple, but it might take you a few goes to complete it!

2 Right-click the **touching color?** block you used in your **repeat until** block (or tap and hold on a touchscreen). A menu opens. Choose **Duplicate**

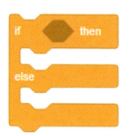

 3 As you move the mouse, a copy of the **touching color?** block moves with it. Click over the diamond-shaped hole of the **if... then... else** block to drop the block in. On a touchscreen, the new block appears in the Code Area. You can then drag it into the **if... then... else** block

...cont'd

4 Click the **Looks** button beside the Blocks Palette. Drag a **say Hello! for 2 seconds** block into both of the brackets in your **if... then... else** block

5 This **say** block displays a message in a speech bubble. After 2 seconds, it disappears again. Click the "Hello!" text in the first **say** block, and change it to "Ouch!". Change the text in the second **say** block to "Hurrah! You won!". The way the **if... then... else** block works is that it checks whether something is true, and if it is, it runs the blocks in its first bracket, and otherwise it runs the blocks in its second bracket. We're checking whether the fish has hit the spiral, so if it has, the first **say** block will display the message for losing the game. If the fish isn't touching the spiral, it must be touching the crab at this point in the script, so the program shows the congratulations message

6 Your final script is shown on the right. It keeps the fish moving until it hits the crab or the spiral, and then displays one message if it hit the spiral, and a different message otherwise

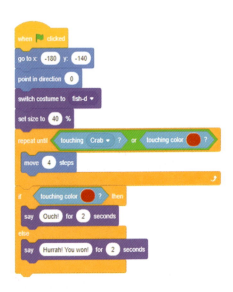

4 Super Dodgeball

In this chapter, you'll make a game where you have to dodge bouncing balls and collect ice creams. As you build the game, you'll learn a new way to move sprites, how to make random numbers and use them to add suspense to a game, how to paint your own sprites, and how to clone sprites.

Introducing Super Dodgeball

It can be hard to relax at the seaside with so many other people around, playing games and getting in the way. In Super Dodgeball, you have to avoid all the beachballs bouncing around.

Each time a ball hits you, your strength is sapped. Your energy is shown with a semi-transparent picture of your cat character, which shrinks as your strength decreases.

You score by collecting ice creams that pop up on the screen, but they soon disappear again if you're not quick enough. Ice cream also gives you a small dose of energy, to help you recover from being hit by the beachballs.

In this chapter, you'll learn how to:

- Move sprites in a new way, under keyboard control.

- Design your own sprites.

- Add randomness to your game.

- Copy and clone sprites.

- Add sound effects.

- Adjust the game's difficulty.

If you need more room in the Code Area, reduce the size of the Stage. Above the Stage are three buttons. The first makes the Stage small, the second makes it normal size, and the third one is for full screen.

Setting up the variables

We'll use two variables in this game: one to keep track of the player's score, and one to keep track of the player's percentage strength remaining:

 Click the **Variables** button beside the Blocks Palette

Variables

 Click the **Make a Variable** button in the Blocks Palette

Make a Variable

3 Type **score** into the Variable name box. The standard options are correct for this variable (make the variable for all sprites, and don't make it a cloud variable). That means you can just press Enter or click the **OK** button

New Variable ✖

New variable name:

score|

⦿ For all sprites ○ For this sprite only

☐ Cloud variable (stored on server)

Cancel **OK**

4 Repeat the process, but this time enter the name **strength** to create the *strength* variable

It's a new project, so start with a clean slate. Use the File menu and choose New or click the Create button at the top of the screen to start afresh!

Cloud variables are explained in Chapter 8.

...cont'd

5 When you make variables, reporting boxes are added to the Stage to display their values. They appear in the top-left corner, but you can move them. Click the *score* box and drag it to the top-right corner, and release the mouse button to position it there. We won't use the *strength* box, so you can leave that where it is

Hot tip

Every project begins with a variable called *my variable*. We won't be using it in this project, so feel free to right-click its block (or tap and hold it) so you can delete it.

strength 0

score 0

6 In the Blocks Palette, there are rounded blocks for each of your variables. The checkbox beside them decides whether the variable should be shown on the Stage. We'll show the player's strength using our energy meter instead of the variable box on the Stage, so uncheck the box beside the *strength* variable

my variable

score

strength

Preparing for the game start

Before you start bouncing balls and designing your dream ice cream, there are a few other things you need to prepare:

1 When the game starts, we need to position and size the cat correctly. Beside the Blocks Palette, click the **Events** button. Drag the **when green flag clicked** block into the Code Area

2 Click the **Looks** button beside the Blocks Palette and drag in the **set size to 100%** block. Change the number in it to 50. Shrinking the cat makes it easier to dodge the beachballs, which makes the game more playable

3 Click the **Motion** button. Drag in the **go to x:0 y:0** block. This ensures the cat starts in the middle of the Stage

4 Click the **Variables** button beside the Blocks Palette. Drag in the **set [my variable] to 0** block. Change the variable name in it to *score*. This ensures the score starts at zero each time the game is played

5 Your script should look like this

You might think that some of these blocks are unnecessary because the cat's already in the middle and the score's already zero. But what happens when someone plays twice? The second time around, the score and cat position will carry on from the first game unless you reset them.

You can refer back to the grid reference chart in Chapter 2 if it helps you to visualize how this movement is working.

Last chapter, you used the "when space key pressed" hat block. That's unsuitable for games that need fast fingers, because when you hold down a key, there's a delay before it repeats. Using the Sensing block as we have in this project enables the player to hold down the key to dash across the Stage.

Using coordinates to move

In the last chapter, you learned how to use directions to move a sprite under keyboard control. Spiral Rider used a loop to move the sprite continuously, and used the controls to change its direction.

For this game, we'll use a different technique. Each time an arrow key is pressed, the program will change the sprite's x or y coordinate slightly, making the sprite appear to move.

This is how to use this technique:

- To go right, change the x coordinate by a positive number.

- To go left, change the x coordinate by a negative number.

- To go up, change the y coordinate by a positive number.

- To do down, change the y coordinate by a negative number.

Follow these steps to add the player's movements:

1. Click the **Control** button beside the Blocks Palette (see picture, right)

2. Drag the **forever** block into your cat's script. Join it at the bottom of your script so far

3. Drag the **if** block into your script, and drop it inside your **forever** block

4. Click the **Sensing** button beside the Blocks Palette. It's underneath the Control button (see picture, above)

5. Drag the **key [space] pressed?** block into your script and drop it into the frame of your **if** block. Click the menu to select the **right arrow** key

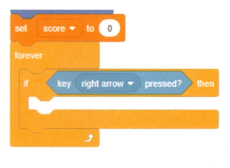

6 Click the **Motion** button beside the Blocks Palette. Drag the **change x by 10** block into the bracket of your **if** block. This block makes the sprite move right by 10 steps and will be used when the right arrow key is pressed

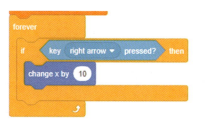

Hot tip

When you duplicate a block, it also duplicates the blocks joined inside or underneath it.

7 Right-click (or tap and hold) the **if** block and select **Duplicate** in the menu. A copy of your **if** bracket and all its contents follows the mouse pointer, or appears in the Code Area on a touch device. Drop it or drag it underneath your original **if** bracket

8 Click the Sensing block in the copy to change the key to the **left arrow** key. Change the number in the **change x by 10** block to -10

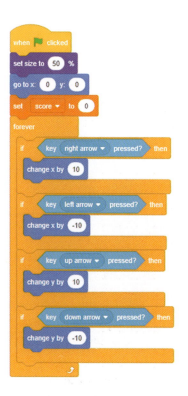

Don't forget

To get rid of a block or script you no longer need in the Code Area, drag it into the Blocks Palette.

9 Repeat this process to add controls for moving up and down. Instead of using the **change x by 10** block, use the **change y by 10** block. Remember, use 10 to go up, and use -10 to go down

10 Test it by clicking the **green flag** and trying the arrow keys. You should see the cat move in four directions

Hot tip

Scratch won't let sprites walk off the edge of the Stage.

Below: Your Stage should look something like this, although it doesn't matter where the sprites are. One of my cats is smaller because I've been testing the movement script, which resizes the player's sprite.

Adding more images

You've already learned how to add sprites to your project (see Chapter 3) and how to change the backdrop (see Chapter 1), so use those skills to add the following:

1 Add the Beachball sprite. You can scroll to find it, or type its name into the search box at the top of the sprite library

2 Add another Cat sprite. It's in the Animals category. We'll use this for the energy meter in the corner of the Stage

3 Add a backdrop. I've chosen Beach Malibu, which is the Outdoors category. You might prefer another outdoor scene, or to set the game indoors

4 Let's rename our sprites to something more meaningful so we can more easily understand which is which. Click the new cat in the Sprite List

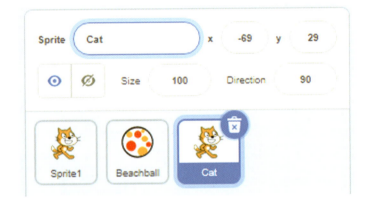

5 Click the box containing the sprite's name above the Sprite List (shown above highlighted in blue). Delete the sprite's name and replace it with the name "Energy"

6 Repeat this process to rename "Sprite1" to "Cat", so the player's moving sprite will be called Cat in our scripts

Making random numbers

A random number is one that the computer picks for you. You give it the lowest and highest numbers in the range you're interested in, and it chooses a number for you, somewhere in that range. To make a dice in Scratch, for example, you'd ask Scratch for a random number between 1 and 6.

One of the Operator blocks is used for making random numbers, and you can drag it into a number space in another block. Follow these steps to position the beachball in a random starting position, and facing a random direction:

1 Click the beachball in the Sprite List, to make sure you're adding scripts to the right sprite. Click the **Code** tab to show the Code Area

2 Drag the **go to random position** Motion block into the Code Area. This block saves you the trouble of asking for random x and y coordinate positions

3 Drag in a Motion block to **point in direction 90**

4 Click the **Operators** button beside the Blocks Palette. Drag the **pick random 1 to 10** block and drop it into the hole for the direction in that **point in direction 90** block

5 Click the numbers in the **pick random** block and change them to -179 and 180

6 Click your script to test the ball goes to a random position and turns to a random direction. You can see the direction number in the panel above the Sprite List

The block to go to a random position is new in Scratch 3.

Making the game unpredictable like this makes it more fun to play repeatedly than it would be if everything was always in the same place.

We could have used a "go to x:0 y:0 block" and put some "pick random" blocks in place of the numbers. That's useful if you only want a random x position, for example, or you want to limit the random position to only part of the screen.

Moving the ball

The script to move the ball uses mostly blocks you've seen before, and just two new ones. Use your random positioning blocks as the starting point for the script to move the ball:

1 Add a **when green flag clicked** block at the top

2 Click the **Looks** button beside the Blocks Palette and drag in the **show** and **go to front layer** blocks. Join these underneath your random positioning blocks. The **go to front layer** block ensures that when the sprite hits the cat, the ball will be in front, so it looks more like a direct hit

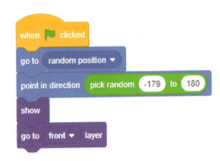

3 Click the **Control** button beside the Blocks Palette and drag in the **wait 1 seconds** and **forever** blocks. Adjust the time delay to 3 seconds. The ball can appear anywhere, so the **wait** block gives the player time to move if the ball appears close to their starting position. The ball doesn't move or sap strength until after that grace period

4 Click the **Motion** button beside the Blocks Palette and drag the **move 10 steps** and **if on edge, bounce** blocks into the **forever** block's bracket. The **if on edge, bounce** block is used to change the direction of the ball when it hits the edge of the Stage

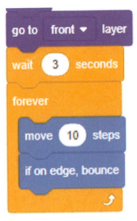

Hot tip

In Shop Cat (see Chapter 10), the "if on edge, bounce" block is used to make cars move left and right across the Stage.

5 Click the **Control** button beside the Blocks Palette and drag in the **if** block. It has to go inside your **forever** bracket

6 Click the **Sensing** button beside the Blocks Palette and drag in the **touching?** block and set it to detect the cat

7 Click the **Variables** button. Drag in the **change [variable name] by 1** block. Click the menu in the block to change the variable to *strength*, and edit the value to -1

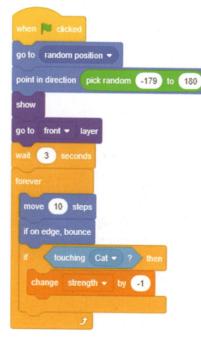

8 Check your finished script against my script on the right here

9 Click the green flag above the Stage and you should see the ball appear in a random location, and start moving in a random direction. You can move the cat, so why not see if you can dodge the ball?

Hot tip

For testing purposes, click the Variables button beside the Blocks Palette and check the box beside strength to show the *strength* variable on the Stage. You should see the number go down as the ball hits the cat. Uncheck the box in the Blocks Palette again to hide the strength.

69

Duplicating sprites is when you make a copy of a sprite while you're writing the game. Cloning is when Scratch makes a copy of a sprite while the game is running.

Hot tip

You might want to delete a sprite, perhaps because you made too many duplicates. Right-click or tap and hold the sprite in the Sprite List, and then choose Delete. To delete a clone of a sprite, use the "delete this clone" block.

Hot tip

For another example of cloning sprites, see Going Batty in Chapter 9.

Copying and cloning sprites

Now we've got one ball bouncing around, let's make it a bit more challenging! You could simply copy (or "duplicate") your Beachball sprite, including its scripts, so that when you play the game, you have several balls all bouncing around randomly. To do that, you would right-click (or tap and hold) the sprite in the Sprite List and choose Duplicate in the menu that opens.

A better approach is to clone your sprite. This means that a sprite can make a copy of itself or another sprite while the game is running. This is a more elegant solution than duplicating sprites yourself, for four reasons:

● The program does the donkey work of making the copies, so it saves you time.

● The clones can be made at any time while the game is running, so you can respond to what the player does. You could have monsters or treasure multiplying, for example, depending on what the player does.

● There's just one set of scripts to edit when you want to make changes. With duplicated sprites, you would have to make changes to the scripts on all of them, if you wanted to change the speed of the balls, for example. With cloned sprites, there's just one sprite to change and the copies of that are made during the game.

● It's easier to understand how the program works, because there are no identical scripts in the program while you're editing it.

There are three Control blocks that are used for managing clones:

● **create clone of myself**: This block creates a copy of the sprite. It also enables you to create a copy of another sprite by clicking the menu in the block and choosing another sprite.

● **when I start as a clone**: This hat block is used at the top of a script you would like to run when the clone is created.

● **delete this clone**: This block is used to delete a clone. No other block can be joined underneath it.

...cont'd

Let's use cloning to make three beachballs appear.

1 Click the beachball in the Sprite List. In the Code Area, remove the **when green flag clicked** hat block from your script. To do this, click the second block in the stack (the **go to** block), and drag it away from the hat block. Keep the **when green flag clicked** block in the Code Area

Hot tip

Click the green flag to see three beachballs bouncing around. You can practice dodging them, although there is no penalty when you're hit yet.

2 Click the **Control** button beside the Blocks Palette. Drag in the **when I start as a clone** hat block, and join this to the top of your script

```
when I start as a clone
go to   random position ▼
point in direction   pick random  -179  to  180
show
```

3 Add the blocks shown here to the **when green flag clicked** block. You can find the **hide** block by clicking the **Looks** button beside the Blocks Palette. The rest are Control blocks

Hot tip

You can change the wait time to adjust how long there is before each ball appears, and you can increase the number of balls by changing the number of times the loop that creates them repeats. Cloning makes it simple to make changes like this, which would be quite fiddly if you were using duplicated sprites instead.

The **hide** block is there because the original beachball is only used to make copies of itself. It's the clones that do the bouncing. When the green flag is clicked, the beachball makes three clones of itself, 10 seconds apart. When each clone is created, it uses the same script you used previously to move to a random position, pause briefly and then start bouncing around.

Scratch makes it easy to have several sprites doing different things at once. In this program, the energy meter is always adjusting its size to match the *strength* variable and checking whether to end the game. At the same time, the balls are bouncing and the player is moving. Each sprite can have a script that starts when the green flag is clicked.

72

Above: The energy meter's ghost effect means the backdrop shines through.

Adding the energy meter

We're going to show the player how much energy they have left using an energy meter, which is a picture of the player's character (the cat), that changes its size as the player loses or gains energy:

1 Click the Energy sprite in the Sprite List to select it

2 Beside the Blocks Palette, click the **Events** button. Drag the **when green flag clicked** block into the Code Area

3 Click the **Variables** button beside the Blocks Palette

4 Drag in the **set [variable name] to 0** block and join it to the **when green flag clicked** block. Change the variable name in the block to *strength*, and the number to 100. This ensures the strength is set to its maximum value as the game starts

5 Click the **Motion** button beside the Blocks Palette and drag in the **go to x:0 y:0** block. Change the numbers in it to x:-190 and y:120. This puts the energy meter in the top-left corner of the screen

6 Click the **Looks** button beside the Blocks Palette and drag in the **set color effect to 0** block. Change the effect to ghost, and the number to 50. This makes our energy meter semi-transparent, so it doesn't look like a character in the game (see Figure 1, facing page)

7 Click the **Control** button beside the Blocks Palette. Drag in the **forever** block, and add an **if** block inside its bracket (see Figure 2, facing page)

8 The **if** block is used to check whether the player has run out of strength, which will be when the *strength* variable is less than 1. Click the **Operators** button beside the Blocks Palette and drag the **<** block into the **if** block (see Figure 3, facing page). This checks whether the number on the left is less than the number on the right. It has a 50 on the right until you change it

9 Click the **Variables** button beside the Blocks Palette. Drag the *strength* variable block into the left of the Operator block. Type a 1 into the right of that block. This will check whether the strength is less than 1, and will do whatever is inside the **if** bracket if it is

10 Click the **Looks** button beside the Blocks Palette and drag the **say Hello! for 2 seconds** block into the **if** bracket. Change the text in it to "Game Over"

11 Click the **Control** button beside the Blocks Palette and drag the **stop all** block into the **if** bracket. This will stop the game if the *strength* variable is less than 1

12 Finally, you need to make the energy meter change its size. Click the **Looks** button beside the Blocks Palette and drag in the **set size to 100%** block. It goes inside the **forever** bracket, but outside the **if** bracket. Click **Variables** beside the Blocks Palette, and drag the *strength* variable block into its number space (see Figure 4, right)

Fig 1
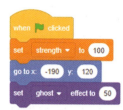

Fig 2

Fig 3
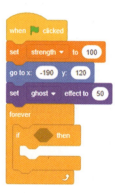

Fig 4
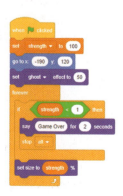

Beware

If you just check whether *strength* is equal to zero, the game might never end. A ball could be sapping the player's energy, and could take the *strength* variable into negative numbers before the program checked whether the strength was zero and stopped the game.

Hot tip

After you've added the energy meter, play the game to test it. The meter should shrink as the ball hits the player, and when it disappears completely, the game should end.

Painting in Scratch

Scratch includes a Paint Editor you can use to design your own sprites and backdrops, or to edit the existing ones. There isn't an ice cream sprite provided with Scratch, so you'll need to use the Paint Editor to make one for the Super Dodgeball game.

To create a new sprite, hover over (or tap) the **new sprite** button in the Sprite List. Click the **Paint new sprite** button, which looks like a paintbrush.

The Paint Editor (see facing page) uses vector art. That means you can edit the shapes and lines that make up your picture later.

Down the left of the canvas, you can see the tools you can use to make your sprite costume. Click a tool to select it. The tools are:

- **Select**: Click a shape in your image to select it, or hold down Shift and click to select several. You can then rotate your selection by clicking and holding the rotation control at the bottom of the selected area and moving your mouse. You can stretch or squeeze the shape by dragging the markers on the corners or the sides of the selected shape. To move the shape, click it and drag it.

- **Reshape**: This tool enables you to click a point on a shape and adjust it. You can drag it in and out. The handles that extend out of the point on both sides are used to change the angle of the line entering that point. You can click the outline anywhere to add a new reshaping point. Use the button above the canvas to switch between a curved or pointed line. The best way to understand this tool is to experiment with it, so why not give it a go?

Hot tip

You can use the Paint Editor to customize the sprites that come with Scratch too. Click your sprite in the Sprite List to select it, then click the Costumes tab above the Blocks Palette.

NEW

The vector editor is now the normal art editor in Scratch 3, replacing the bitmap editor as the default option.

Beware

When using Scratch online, your changes are saved automatically. If you want to play around with the Paint Editor, start a new sprite, rather than editing one you will need later.

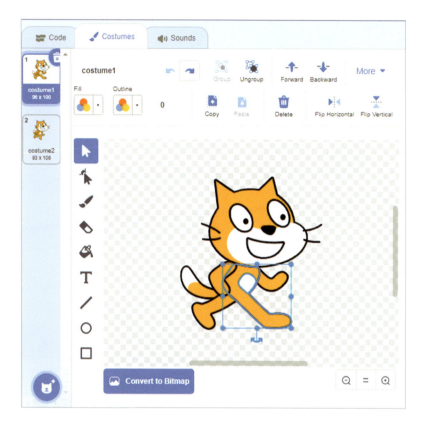

You can use buttons above the canvas to copy and paste, or flip a selected shape.

Hot tip

Vector art is great for creating animations. You can right-click a costume in the Costumes Area and duplicate it. You can easily make multiple animation frames by tweaking the vector art, and then use the "next costume" block to switch between them. Try editing the cat's costume to reposition or extend its legs, or try tilting its head.

Hot tip

The checkered pattern on the canvas represents transparency, where the backdrop will show through your sprite.

- **Brush**: Simply hold down the mouse button as you move your pointer over the canvas, and you leave a line behind you. Choose the thickness and color above the canvas.

- **Eraser**: Removes part of your shape. Choose the size of the eraser in the options above the canvas.

- **Fill**: This will fill a shape on your image with color. In the options area above the canvas, you can choose your color.

- **Text**: This tool enables you to write on the canvas with a choice of several fonts, including Sans Serif, Serif, Handwriting, Marker, Curly, and Pixel. Use Enter to start a new line when you're typing your text. In the options area above the canvas, you can change the font and color. Adjust the size of your text using the handles on the side of the box around the text. You can also use the Select tool to reposition and resize your text after you've created it. Double-click your text to edit it.

...cont'd

There is also a bitmap editor, which is good for pixel art, inspired by classic arcade games. While there are tools you can use to draw shapes in this mode, you're basically coloring in dots on the canvas. Images may be lower quality, and will be harder to edit. To access bitmap mode, click Convert to Bitmap under the canvas.

In the color palette, the white box with a red line through it represents transparent ink.

If you hold down the Shift key while you're creating a rectangle, the tool creates a perfect square. To make a perfect circle, hold down the Shift key while using the Circle tool.

- **Line**: Click at the start of the line, hold the mouse button down, and move to the end of the line. When you release the mouse button, a straight line is drawn between where you clicked and where you released the mouse button. Above the canvas, choose the (outline) color and thickness of the line.

- **Circle**: Click, hold down the mouse button and drag the mouse pointer to create a circle or ellipse. The shape expands to fill the space between where you click and where you release the mouse button. Above the canvas, you can choose the fill color (inside the shape), the outline color (around the edge), and the thickness of the line.

- **Rectangle**: Click to position one corner, hold the mouse button down, and then drag to the opposite corner and release the button. In the options, you can choose the fill and outline colors, and the line thickness.

Using the options above the canvas

The options above the canvas (see below) include:

- **Rename costume**: Enter a new costume name in the top left.

- **Undo/Redo**: If you make a mistake, click the **Undo** button (a curved arrow pointing left). To reinstate your change, click the **Redo** button beside it.

- **Group/Ungroup**: You can combine shapes to edit them as one object. The Scratch cat, for example, has all the head elements grouped as one. Select and ungroup the head if you want to move an eye, but not the rest of the head.

- **Forward/Backward, Front/Back**: Use these options to control which shapes appear in front of others. Select a shape and use Forward/Backward to move through the layers, and Front/Back to move a shape to the very front or back.

Undo/Redo

Creating the ice cream

Let's use the Paint Editor to create an ice cream sprite.

1 Click the button to paint a new sprite

2 Choose the Circle tool beside the canvas. Hold down the Shift key and click and drag with the mouse to draw a perfect circle. Draw two more of a similar size

3 Click the Select tool and drag the circles so they form a cluster, with two at the bottom and one balancing on the top

4 Because you're using vector art, you can edit shapes after you've created them. We can now click each of the circles and choose a different fill color for it. The color options enable you to choose a color, saturation and brightness. To get white, you would turn Saturation all the way down and Brightness all the way up. For black, you would choose the minimum brightness. For our ice cream, we want three bright colors for different fruit flavors. Experiment with the sliders to find colors you like. You can also click the pipette in the color options to choose a color from the Stage. At the top of the color panel are three options for a graduated fill, which enables you to fade one color into another. A solid fill works fine for our purposes here

5 Select the Line tool. Draw a triangle, making sure the lines join up. Select the Fill tool. Pick a color for your wafer cone, and click the triangle to fill it

6 Use the Select tool and the **Forward/Backward** buttons to arrange the cone and the ice cream scoops as you wish

7 In the Sprite List, rename your sprite to "ice cream"

Hot tip

In the middle of the canvas are tiny crosshairs. Try to design your sprite so its center is on this crosshair, or move your image there afterwards. It doesn't matter so much in this game, but in others your sprite might seem to move strangely if Scratch thinks the center is not where the middle of your image is. Previous versions of Scratch had a button to set the costume center wherever you want. It's expected to be added to the current version in the future.

Above: My finished ice cream sprite.

If you don't want to design your own sprite, you can use one of the sprites that come with Scratch to finish this game. They include the healthier food options of bananas, apples and oranges.

To get back to your scripts, click the Code tab above the Costumes Area.

The "go to random position" block is new in Scratch 3.

Making the ice cream appear

After all that hard work, you deserve an ice cream! You need to add two scripts to the ice cream sprite: this first one makes it appear in random locations for a short while and then disappear:

1 Drag in the **when green flag clicked** block. I'm sure you know where to find it by now! It's an Events block

2 Click the **Looks** button beside the Blocks Palette. Drag in the **go to front** and **go forward 1 layers** blocks. Use the menu to choose to go backward 1 layer instead. This means the ice cream will appear behind the beachballs, which looks most natural

3 It's easier to draw sprites large, so my ice cream sprite was huge. I used the **set size** block to reduce its size to 30%. You can use a similar block, and adjust the size to what you need

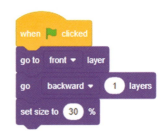

4 Click the **Control** button beside the Blocks Palette and drag the **forever** block into your script

5 Click the **Motion** button beside the Blocks Palette and add the **go to random position** block. If you click this script to run it now, you'll see the ice cream flicker all over the Stage, as it moves much too quickly for the cat to catch it

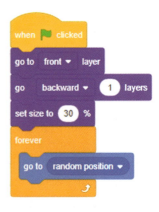

6 Click the **Looks** button beside the Blocks Palette and drag the **show** and **hide** blocks into your script as shown on the right of this page

7 Click the **Control** button beside the Blocks Palette and drag two **wait 1 seconds** blocks into your script, after each of the **show** and **hide** blocks

8 Click the **Operators** button beside the Blocks Palette and drag a **pick random 1 to 10** block into each of the wait blocks. Adjust the numbers in the **pick random** blocks, so the ice cream is shown for between 5 and 10 seconds, and hidden for between 1 and 3 seconds

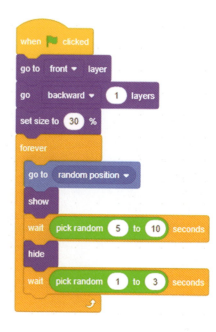

Hot tip

The ice cream in Super Dodgeball not only provides a scoring mechanism and a way to replenish strength. It also forces players to move around the screen, so they can't just find a safe place and stay there!

Enabling the player to score

The other script you need to add to your ice cream detects when the player reaches it, and then increases the score and strength:

1 Drag in the **when green flag clicked** block

2 Click the **Control** button beside the Blocks Palette and drag the **forever** block into your script

3 Add the **wait until** block into your script. It's another Control block

A sprite can have more than one script triggered by the green flag. We're using two on the ice cream.

4 Click the **Sensing** button beside the Blocks Palette. Drag the **touching?** block into the space in your **wait until** block, and then click the menu in it to choose the cat. This block will pause this script until the cat is touching the ice cream

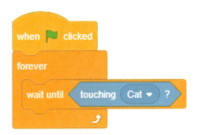

5 If the cat's touching the ice cream, we need to increase the *score* and the *strength* variables! Click the **Variables** button beside the Blocks Palette. Drag in two copies of the **change [variable name] by 1** block. Click the menu in the blocks to choose the *strength* and *score* variables, and change the number to 10 in both blocks

6 At the moment, it's possible for the player's strength to be more than 100, if they collect an ice cream before being hit by a ball, for example. We need to make sure the strength doesn't go above 100. Click the **Control** button beside the Blocks Palette and drag in the **if** block

7 Click the **Operators** button beside the Blocks Palette, and drag the > block into the space in the **if** block

8 Click the **Variables** button beside the Blocks Palette. Drag the *strength* variable into the left of the > block, and type 100 in the right of it, replacing the 50 there already

9 Drag the **set [variable name] to 0** block into the bracket of the **if** block. Change the variable in it to *strength*, and the value in it to 100. That will ensure that if the *strength* variable is higher than 100, it is set to be exactly 100

10 Finally, click the **Looks** button beside the Blocks Palette and drag the **hide** block into the end of your **forever** loop. This will hide the ice cream if the cat touches it, making it look like the cat has picked it up. The other script on the ice cream continues to run, so the ice cream will reappear somewhere new after a random period of time

The > Operator block checks whether the number on the left is higher than the number on the right.

If you need to stop a variable going above or below a certain value in your own game, you can modify the blocks used here to do that.

Some of these ideas can be used in other Scratch games you make too.

Hot tip

Don't be afraid to experiment and see what happens if you change numbers around, or add in your own effects. Click File and choose "Save as a copy", and your project will be saved with a new name, leaving the previous version untouched. If your game stops working, you can always go back to the previous version you made.

Tweaking the gameplay

If you find the game is too easy or too difficult, there are several things you can do to adjust the speed and difficulty of the game:

- To slow down the ball, change the number in its **move 10 steps** block to a lower number.

- To speed up the ball, change the number in its **move 10 steps** block to a higher number.

- To give players more time to react when a ball appears near them, change the number in the **wait 3 seconds** block to a higher number.

- To make it easier to dodge the balls, make them smaller. You can do this by adding a **set size to 100%** block under the **when green flag clicked** block in their scripts. Change the number from 100% to something smaller.

- To make it easier to catch the ice cream, make it bigger. Change the number in its **set size to 30% block** to a greater number.

- To make the game harder, you could stop the ice cream replenishing the player's strength, or make it increase the strength by less than 10.

- To give players more time to catch the ice cream, you can adjust the random numbers used to decide how long it's on screen. After its **show** block, change the random waiting time to a minimum of 10 seconds and a maximum of 20 seconds, to give players at least 10 seconds to catch it.

- To make the energy last twice as long, change how much energy the ball saps when it touches the cat from 1 to 0.5. Click the ball sprite and edit the **change strength by -1** block to **change strength by -0.5**.

When you design games, you'll often find you need to adjust things like this to make the difficulty just right: a bit challenging, but not so difficult that it's not fun to play.

Professional game designers get other people to test their games, and watch them to see how easy or difficult they find them. Lots of people who use Scratch put their games on the Scratch website for others to try and give them feedback on too (see Chapter 11).

5 Space Opera

In this chapter, you get to conduct an alien opera performance, triggering samples and musical notes. You'll learn how to add sound effects and musical notes to your projects. You'll also learn how you can use Scratch to compose music or play your favorite tunes.

Introducing Space Opera

In Space Opera, you conduct an operatic alien singer, and can jam along on the keyboards, guitar and drum. You use the top row of letter keys (from Q to I) to control which notes the guitar plays, and click the other instruments to play them. The keyboard note varies depending on which part of the keyboard you click, with low notes on the left and high notes on the right. The singer sings a lower note than the previous one if you click them on their left, and a higher note than the previous one if you click them on their right. You can make up tunes by clicking on their left and right hands in different patterns.

This project teaches you some important Scratch techniques:

- Two different ways to make music, by playing short recordings, and by playing notes using simulated instruments.

- How to use graphic effects to change a sprite's appearance.

- How to animate a sprite using multiple costumes.

Now that you've completed several Scratch projects, you're an expert on the basics. In this chapter, I'll assume that you know how to add blocks to a script, and where to find the blocks you've used often before, such as the **when green flag clicked** block, and the **go to x:0 y:0** block.

This project mostly works fine on touch devices. The guitar needs a computer keyboard, though, so you might prefer to leave the guitar out if you don't have a computer keyboard.

Playing sounds

Click the **Sound** button beside the Blocks Palette to find these blocks:

- **play sound [sound name] until done**: This block plays your sound but waits until it's finished before the next block in the script runs. Choose a different sound using the menu in the block.

- **start sound [sound name]**: Use this block to start a sound. The script moves to the next block while the sound plays.

- **stop all sounds**: This block stops the sounds playing on all sprites. It doesn't stop the notes and drums you'll learn about later in the Music extension.

- **change [pitch] effect by 10**: Use this block to make all the sound effects on a sprite higher in pitch. Use a negative number to make them lower. An increase of 10 is equivalent to going up one key on the piano. In this block you can also choose the pan effect, which controls whether the sounds seem to come from the left or the right. Use negative numbers to move to the left, and positive for the right.

- **set [pitch] effect to 100**: Set the pitch effect or pan effect. The pan numbers range from -100 (left) to +100 (right).

- **clear sound effects**: Clears the pitch and pan effects.

- **change volume by -10**: This block turns the volume down by 10%. You can change the number in the block, and make it a positive number to increase the volume. The volume affects the sounds and the Music extension blocks.

- **set volume to 100%**: Change the number in this block to set the volume to your chosen level.

- **volume**: This is a variable that contains the current volume level, from 0 to 100.

There's a shortcut in the menu in the "play sound" and "start sound" blocks that you can use to record a new sound.

The sound effects blocks are new in Scratch 3.

Adding the electric guitar

Above: The electric guitar sprite we're adding.

Let's add our first instrument to this project, the electric guitar

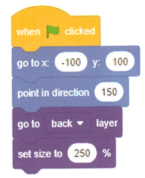

1 Delete the Cat sprite

2 Change the backdrop to Space City 2

3 Add the Guitar-electric2 sprite from the library

4 Add the script above to the guitar. It puts the guitar in the top left of the Stage

5 Add the scripts shown at the bottom of this page to the guitar sprite too

6 Click the green flag, and use the keys Q to I to play music!

Don't forget

To find these "start sound" blocks, click the Sound button to the left of the Blocks Palette.

Hot tip

The guitar sprite includes sound recordings of musical notes. These are the sounds we're playing in our scripts.

Using costumes

Each sprite can have more than one picture, or "costume". You use them to change the appearance of a sprite using blocks.

1 Add the Drum-snare sprite to your project

2 Above the Blocks Palette, click the **Costumes** tab

3 The Costumes Area shows you the two costumes for the drum. Underneath each one is its name (e.g. drum-snare-a) and size (44 units wide by 66 high). On the right is the Paint Editor (the checkered area), so you can redesign the costume. Here, we can see that our silent drum is called drum-snare-a and the one with drumsticks playing is drum-snare-b

4 In the Looks part of the Blocks Palette, you can find the block to switch costumes

5 You can also use the **next costume** block. It moves to the next costume in the sequence. After it's shown the last costume, it goes back to the first one. This block is ideal for animations, such as making the cat's legs move each time it takes a step

Hot tip

To delete a costume, click it in the Costumes Area, and then click the trash can in the top-right corner of the costume. You aren't prompted to confirm, but you can go to the Edit menu and click Restore Costume if you make a mistake.

Hot tip

To add another costume to your sprite, use the round Choose a Costume button in the bottom-left of the Costumes Area. You can add a costume from the library, paint one, upload a picture from your computer or use your webcam to take a picture.

Adding graphic effects

Scratch includes a number of graphic effects you can apply to the backdrop and your sprites. They are:

- **color,** which changes the sprite's color palette.

- **fisheye**, which distorts like a fisheye camera lens, with central parts of the image being magnified.

- **whirl**, which twists the picture around its middle, like water circling a drain.

- **pixelate**, which makes the picture blockier.

- **mosaic**, which turns the image into lots of small tiles of itself.

- **brightness**, which adjusts the brightness of the sprite's colors.

- **ghost**, which makes the sprite semi-transparent.

Three blocks are used to manage these effects. You can find them all in the Looks section of the Blocks Palette:

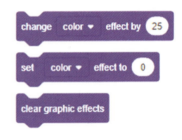

- **change color effect by 25**: Click the menu in the block to change the effect from color to one of the others. Click to edit the number. You can use negative numbers too.

- **set color effect to 0**: This block resets the chosen effect.

- **clear graphic effects**: This block resets all graphic effects.

Hot tip

As you might expect, you can change the number in the "set color effect to 0" block. To go straight to 50% color effect, use 50 here, for example.

Hot tip

It's worth playing around with the graphic effects to see how you can use them in your programs.

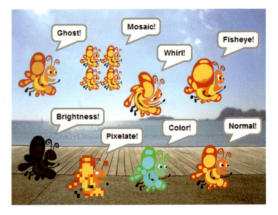

Right: Showing the color effects. The brightness effect is using a negative number here to darken the sprite.

Adding the drum

Let's add some scripts to our drum to enable you to play it, and see an animated effect when you do.

1 Click the drum sprite in the Sprite List

2 Add this script to the sprite. It positions your drum in the top right. Things might look a bit spaced out now (ahem!), but we'll fill the Stage with more sprites later

Hot tip

As you saw in Spiral Rider, you can add scripts to the Stage too. Try this script to make it slowly change color, as if under concert lighting.

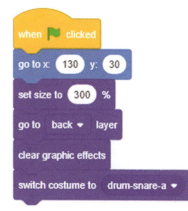

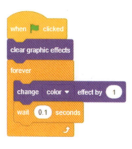

3 Add this script to the drum sprite too. It uses the new costume and graphic effects blocks to animate the drum

Below: When you click the drum, it changes to the costume showing the drumsticks and swells using the fisheye effect. When the sound finishes, it switches to the normal costume, and the graphic effect is cleared.

Adding the singer

We're going to add a singer now, who sings a lower note than the last one if you click on their left, and a higher note than the last one if you click on their right.

1 Add the Kiran sprite to your project

2 Click the **Sounds** tab above the Code Area

3 Hover over the button in the bottom left to add a sound. You can choose a sound from the library, record one or upload a sound from your computer

4 The sound library is similar to the sprite library you've seen already. You can search for a sound by name, browse them all, or explore a particular category. Loops are fragments of music that you can repeat to make a continuous tune or drum pattern. The Notes category includes notes and chords recorded with a guitar, bass guitar, piano, saxophone, trumpet, and trombone

5 Add the sound Singer2 to your sprite. This is a single, high note sung in an operatic style. Find it by name

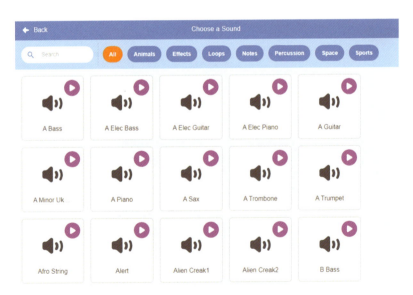

6 The Sounds Area includes tools for editing your sound. Select a sound on the left. You can then apply effects such as fade in, fade out, reverse, or robot by clicking them underneath the soundwave. Press Play to hear what it sounds like. Use the **Undo** button above the soundwave (a curved arrow to the left) if you make a mistake

Hot tip

The "mouse x" and "mouse y" blocks are Sensing blocks. They give you the coordinates of the mouse pointer on the Stage.

mouse x

mouse y

7 Add the scripts below to your Kiran sprite. The one on the left positions Kiran. The one on the right uses the mouse position to work out whether to make the pitch higher or lower before playing the sound. Because Kiran's x position is 0, if the mouse x position is less than 0, that means it's on Kiran's left, otherwise it's on Kiran's right

```
when [flag] clicked
go to x: 0 y: 50
go to back ▼ layer
go forward ▼ 1 layers
switch costume to kiran-a ▼
```

```
when this sprite clicked
switch costume to kiran-b ▼
if  mouse x  < 0  then
    change pitch ▼ effect by -10
else
    change pitch ▼ effect by 10

play sound Singer2 ▼ until done
switch costume to kiran-a ▼
```

Below: Kiran comes with six costumes. We're just using the first two. The open-mouthed one (kiran-b) is used when singing.

Playing music in Scratch

As well as playing sound recordings, you can program Scratch to generate music using drums and simulated instruments. The blocks to do this are all in the Music extension. Whether you know how to make music already or not, you can use Scratch to write your own tunes with these blocks:

The Music blocks are an extension. Add them using the Add Extension button in the bottom left of the Blocks Palette.

Music
Play instruments and drums.

- **play drum [name] for 0.25 beats**: You can click the name to open a menu and choose a different type of drum. This block only plays the drum once, but you can change how many beats (or how much time) that drum takes up.

- **rest for 0.25 beats**: Use this block to add a short silence (a rest) in your music.

- **play note 60 for 0.25 beats**: The number 60 is for the note known as middle C. Higher numbers are higher notes, and lower numbers are lower notes. Click the 60 to open a menu that helps you choose the note by its name. This includes a piano you can use to choose a note.

- **set instrument to [name]**: Click the name to choose from 21 simulated instruments. Instrument 1 is the piano.

- **set tempo to 60**: This sets the tempo (or speed) of your music at 60 beats per minute (BPM).

- **change tempo by 20**: Use this block to make your music faster, or use a negative number to slow it down.

- **tempo**: You can use this variable to find out what the current tempo (speed) of the music is.

Below: Clicking the note number opens a piano keyboard you can use to select the note.

Adding the synthesizer

We'll add a synthesizer to the Stage that you can click or tap to play a note. Using the x position of the mouse, the script can work out what note to play.

 1 Add the Keyboard sprite to your project

2 Add the Music blocks using the **Add Extension** button in the bottom left of the Blocks Palette

3 Make a variable called *note to play*. Uncheck beside its block

4 Add these two scripts to your keyboard. The first one positions it at the bottom of the Stage and selects the instrument we'll use with it. The second script plays a note when you click the sprite. It works out which note to play, switches to a costume with notes coming out, and changes the color of the keyboard, which looks like concert lighting

5 Try it! Now you can click along the keyboard image to play different notes, use the (real) keys Q to I to play the guitar, click Kiran's hands to make up a tune, and bang the drum

Hot tip

The x coordinates on the stage go from -240 to +240. To turn the mouse position into a useful musical note number, we first add 240 to make a positive number between 0 and 480. Then we divide that by 8, giving us a range of 0 to 60. The "round" block rounds the result to a whole number if it has a decimal part.

93

Hot tip

This project uses the layer blocks to position the guitar at the back, Kiran in front of it, and the keyboard right at the front.

Making your own tunes

You can use what you've learned in this chapter to write your own music with Scratch, or to write programs that play your favorite tunes. There's lots of sheet music available online for free, and you can use it to work out the numbers you need for your **play note** blocks.

It doesn't matter if you don't know how to read music. You can go a long way by knowing a few basics. The five lines in sheet music are called a staff (a stave in the UK). Music often has a treble stave (the higher one) and a bass staff (the lower one), and you can tell which is which from the symbol at the start of it. Each spot on the staff represents one note, and either sits on a line or in a space. Musicians read the music from left to right. A note's vertical position on the staff tells them its pitch (how high or low the note is), and the shape of the note tells them how long it lasts.

Note names and numbers
Where there is a note displayed in both staves below, one above the other, they represent the same note.

Hot tip

If your sheet music has two notes in the same horizontal position on the staff, they're supposed to be played at the same time. You can get Scratch to play two notes at once if you put them in different scripts and trigger them at the same time, perhaps using a broadcast (see page 103 in Chapter 6), but for simple tunes it's easier to just use one of the notes: whichever sounds better.

Hot tip

To write your own music, just experiment with these note numbers. If you're a beginner, I recommend starting and ending on one of the C notes, avoiding big leaps from one note to the next, and making every group of four notes add up to a total of 4 beats.

Note durations

As you know, the shape of the notes (whether they're filled or hollow, whether they have a line on them and so on) tells you how many beats the note lasts. If you're using the time signature 4/4 (sometimes shown with a symbol like a large C at the start of the stave), the most common note durations are:

Name	Note length	Duration	Style
semibreve	whole note	4 beats	
minim	half note	2 beats	
crotchet	quarter note	1 beat	
quaver	one-eighth note	0.5 beat	
semiquaver	one-sixteenth note	0.25 beat	

If there's a dot after the note, it's half as long again. So a dotted minim is 3 beats:

To make a note sharp, add 1 to its note number. To make it flat, subtract 1. Sharp notes are indicated with a symbol like a # sign. Flat notes are shown with a symbol like a lowercase b before them. They usually apply to each use of the same note until you reach the next bar line (a vertical line down the stave). If they're at the start of the stave without a note, they apply to all the notes in that line or space of the stave.

Rests

Music also includes moments of silence, of course, and these are the "rests" between the notes. Here are the symbols you might see for various rests. Remember you can use the **rest for 0.25 beats** block to add these:

Name	Rest length	Duration	Style
semibreve	whole rest	4 beats	
minim	half rest	2 beats	
crotchet	quarter rest	1 beat	
quaver	one-eighth rest	0.5 beat	
semiquaver	one-sixteenth rest	0.25 beat	

It doesn't matter whether the lines on the notes go up or down. If you have notes next to each other that have checkmarks on their lines, they're usually joined up.

Above: The first phrase of the sheet music from the tune. Each note has become one block in the program, making up the first big chunk of music blocks. I've chosen to play the tune one octave lower because it sounds better.

London Bridge

As an example of how you can make music with Scratch, here's a program that plays the traditional tune "London Bridge is Falling Down".

1 The tune includes a bit that repeats. Click the **Variables** button beside the Blocks Palette and make the variable *verse*. Our program uses this to remember whether it's the first or second time it's gone around its loop. The first time, it plays six additional notes

2 To play the tune, add the script (right) to your sprite

3 Click the **green flag** button to hear the tune

4 You can customize this program by changing the instrument played to something else, and experimenting with different notes

Your games could start or end with a tune played like this.

6 Quiz Break

Can you beat the clock? In Quiz Break, you are challenged to answer 10 maths questions in an average of three seconds each. If you do it, the quizmaster dances. In this project, you'll learn how to use the timer, ask the player questions, and join text in speech bubbles.

You can play this game using a tablet. I recommend using portrait orientation. Tap the answer box to see your keyboard. You can adjust the difficulty if you find it too hard to answer quickly on a tablet.

Introducing Quiz Break

In recent years, games based on speed mathematics have become popular on handheld consoles and phones. They're a good warm-up for your brain, as well as being itchingly, frustratingly good fun.

In the game Quiz Break, you're challenged to answer simple mathematics questions against the clock. If you can answer 10 questions quickly enough, your host will be so impressed he'll dance for you. You don't get that on TV quiz shows!

In this chapter, you'll learn how to:

● Ask the player questions.

● Use a timer to measure how long the player is taking.

● Use broadcasts to coordinate actions between sprites.

● Use the Operators blocks to perform calculations.

● Join pieces of text together so you can make sprites say more complex sentences in their speech bubbles.

To complete this project, you'll draw on what you've learned in previous chapters, including using the pen (see Chapter 2), variables (see Chapter 3), random numbers (see Chapter 4), and multiple costumes (see Chapter 5).

This game is set up to test your multiplication tables, but you can easily make it test addition, subtraction or division by changing the Operator blocks used.

Preparing for Quiz Break

To get ready to make this game, follow these steps:

1 Start a new project and add the Metro backdrop. It's in the Outdoors category

2 Add the sprite Champ99. He's in the People category. This sprite includes several costumes we can use to animate a dance. If you prefer, you could choose Anina Dance or Cassy Dance

Champ99

3 Select the cat in the Sprite List and then click the trash can icon on its corner to delete it from the project. We don't need the cat sprite in this game

Sprite1   Champ99

4 Click the **Variables** button beside the Blocks Palette and make six variables with the following names: *average*, *number1*, *number2*, *question*, *time taken*, and *total*. The variable *time taken* must be set up for all sprites for the game to work. For simplicity, set up the others for all sprites too, although only the dancer needs to use the other variables

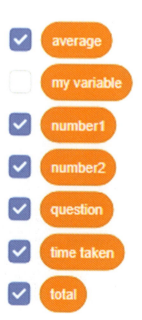

5 Right-click the block for *my variable* and delete it. We don't need it in this project

...cont'd

Don't forget

Sounds can only be played on the sprite they are added to.

Hot tip

We could also have unchecked the variables in the Blocks Palette to hide them. I've used blocks to do the same job here.

Beware

Whenever you have blocks with a menu in, such as these blocks to hide a variable, remember to select the right value in the menu.

6 Click the dancer and add the sound Human Beatbox1 from the Loops category. It's the first loop labeled "Human Be..."

7 Your Stage should look like the picture below. If you chose a different dancer, you'll see him or her on the Stage instead of Champ99

8 At the start of the game, you need to hide the variables on the Stage, switch to the costume that shows the dancer standing upright, and move the dancer to the left of the Stage. Add this script to the dancer sprite. If you are using a different sprite to me, you'll need to change the costume names to those that work best for you

Drawing the timer

To pile on the pressure and give players a visual clue as to how well they're doing, let's add a clock in the top-right corner:

1 Add the Arrow1 sprite. It'll be our clock hand

2 To draw the outline of the clock, let's use the pen on the arrow sprite. Click the **Add Extension** button in the bottom left of the screen, and then add the Pen extension

3 Click the arrow sprite in the Sprite List to make sure you're adding your script to the right sprite

4 Add the following blocks to the sprite. They position the sprite in the top-right corner of the Stage, and set the pen size. They also set the starting direction as 15 degrees, which ensures the spots line up with the clock points

Don't forget

You can have more than one script on a sprite. In this game, we'll have two scripts on the clock hand: one that is activated when the green flag is clicked, and one that starts the hand moving when the game begins.

If you don't adjust the angle, there's a gap where there should be a spot at the 12 o'clock, 3 o'clock, 6 o'clock, and 9 o'clock positions, as you can see here.

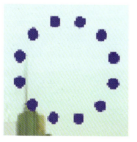

...cont'd

Above: The finished clock.

5 To make the 12 spots on the clock face, draw a dotted dodecagon (a 12-sided shape). Using a thick pen, you can take one step with the pen down to leave a spot, and then move several steps with the pen up to add spacing between the dots. Because we're making 12 spots, we need to turn 30 degrees after each one (30 x 12 = 360 degrees, which completes the circle). Add these blocks to your script (right)

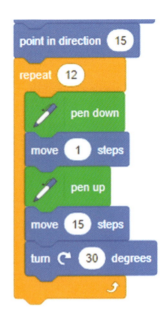

6 To finish, position the arrow in the middle of the clock face (at x:192 y:125) and point it in direction 0, which is up, towards the 12 o'clock position. Add these blocks underneath your repeat loop

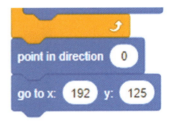

7 Finally, add a block to adjust the size of the sprite to 50%. You can find this purple block in the Looks part of the Blocks Palette. Click the **green flag** to test it!

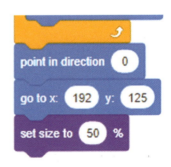

Using broadcasts

You can't make one sprite move or control another sprite, but you can get sprites to cooperate by exchanging messages with each other. That's a much more polite way to do things! These messages are called broadcasts. We'll use them to get the quiz host to start the timer.

There are three Events blocks that are used for managing broadcasts between sprites.

Here's how you use the blocks:

- **broadcast [message]**: This block sends a message out from one sprite to all the other sprites and the backdrop, although you probably won't want them all to respond to that message. You can choose the content of the message, which is just a short piece of text. Click the menu in the block and you can set up a new message, or choose one of the messages you set up previously.

- **when I receive [message]**: This hat block is used to start a script when a certain message is broadcast from any sprite. You can choose which message, or create a new message, from the menu in the block.

- **broadcast [message] and wait**: This block broadcasts a message, but it then waits until any scripts that the message starts have finished. Imagine you used this block to broadcast a message that told a sprite to move. This block would wait until after that sprite had finished moving.

To make it easy to understand your program, set up messages that describe what you're coordinating. It's more meaningful to have a message called "move ship", for example, than "message1".

Hot tip

A sprite can respond to its own broadcast, so you can use broadcasts to trigger actions on all sprites at the same time. If the sprite that sends the broadcast is the only one responding, it might be clearer to make a block instead (see Chapter 7).

Above: When you click the ghost, it makes the cat move. The ghost sends the cat a broadcast to tell it when it's time to move.

Hot tip

Because we used a "broadcast and wait" block, the ghost waits until the cat finishes running before it puts its arms down.

Above: We're using the ghost-a (on the left) and ghost-c costumes (right).

Testing out broadcasts

Here's a simple demonstration you can build to see broadcasts in action. When you click the ghost, it sends a broadcast. The cat receives the broadcast and runs away. Save your quiz game and make this as a new project.

1 Add the Ghost sprite and give it these scripts. Use the menu in the **broadcast [message] and wait** block to create the message "woooh!"

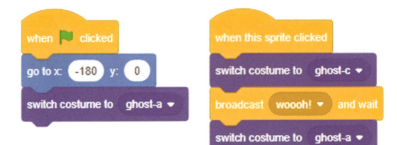

2 Add these scripts to the cat. Click the green flag to position the sprites, then click the ghost

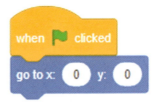
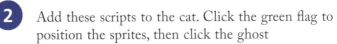

Moving the clock hand

Now, back to the quiz! Scratch has a timer built in to it, and there are two Sensing blocks you can use to work with it:

- **reset timer**: This block sets the timer to zero. The timer is also set to zero when the green flag is clicked.

- **timer**: You can use this block to see how many seconds have passed since the timer was reset. The block is like a variable that you can't change, and you can use it in place of a number in another block. Even after you've clicked the **Stop** button above the Stage, the timer keeps running.

To animate the clock hands, follow these steps:

Click the Sensing button beside the Blocks Palette to find the timing blocks.

1 Click your Arrow1 sprite in the Sprite List, and add the **when I receive [message]** block. It's an Events block. Click the menu in the block and create a new message with the name "start clock". Our dancer will send this message to start the clock ticking

2 Add the **reset timer** block to your script, so the clock always starts with a value of zero, which will translate into the clock hand pointing upwards

3 Add the **repeat until** Control block to your script

...cont'd

The > block is used to check whether the number or variable on the left is higher than the number or variable on the right.

4 We'll use the variable *time taken* to measure how long the player took to answer 10 questions. The clock can use this variable to tell whether the game has finished or not, because its value will be zero until the game ends, and then it will be a number higher than zero. Click the **Operators** button beside the Blocks Palette and drag the > block into the diamond-shaped hole in your **repeat until** block

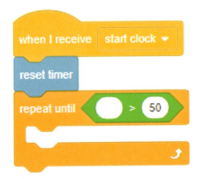

5 Click the **Variables** button beside the Blocks Palette. Drag the *time taken* variable block into the left of your Operator block. Type a number 0 in the hole on the right

NEW

The Operator blocks for comparing numbers have a default value of 50 in them in Scratch 3, instead of both sides being blank. This provides a useful hint about how to use the blocks, but it's easy to forget that you need to replace the value. Remember to change the 50 to 0 here.

6 Inside the bracket of the **repeat until** block, add the **point in direction 90** block

7 Now, you need to change this block so it points the sprite in the right direction, depending on the timer value. The direction is calculated by multiplying the timer (measured in seconds) by 6. That's because we want the hand to do a full circle (360 degrees) in a minute and there are 60 seconds in a minute (60 x 6 = 360). Click the **Operators** button beside the Blocks Palette and drag the rounded block with an asterisk in it into the **point in direction 90** block. The * means multiply

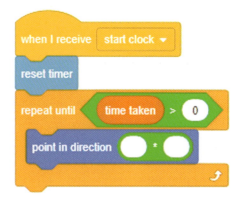

8 Click the **Sensing** button beside the Blocks Palette and drag the **timer** block into one of the holes in your multiplication operator. Type a 6 into the other hole

Hot tip

Check the box beside the "timer" block in the Blocks Palette, and you can see the value of the timer on the Stage. When you're writing a program that uses the timer, this can help you to find out what's causing any errors you experience.

107

Hot tip

Although this script uses a broadcast to trigger it, you can test it by double-clicking it in the Code Area. You should see the hand on your clock turn around, like the second hand on a clock.

Hot tip

You can try different timings for your sound, but should make sure the beats in the notes add up to a total of 1 beat, so that the sound takes 1 second to play before repeating.

Hot tip

Instead of playing a specific note, we're playing the value of a variable here, the timer, and we're adding it to our starting note. As time passes, the note number played is greater and so the tone gets higher. Look out for opportunities like this in your own programs to create sound effects that change as the game is played. You could try playing a sprite's position using the x position or y position Motion blocks, or perhaps play your score variable.

Adding a rising sound effect

To ratchet up the tension, add a sound effect to the clock that gets higher with every passing second:

1 You'll need the Music blocks for this, so use the **Add Extension** button in the bottom left of the screen to add them

2 Click your Arrow1 sprite in the Sprite List

3 Add a broadcast block to start the script when it receives the "start clock" message

4 Add the **set instrument** and **set tempo** blocks. Choose your favorite instrument, and make sure the tempo is set to 60, so there are 60 beats per minute, or 1 per second

5 Add a **repeat until** loop, the same as you used for the script that moves the arrow hand, set to repeat until *time taken* is more than 0

6 Drag in two **play note** blocks. The + Operator block adds two numbers together. Use it to change the note that's played to 36 plus the timer (for three quarters of a beat) and 48 plus the timer (for a quarter of a beat). Tweak the timings, so the first note plays for 0.75 beats and the second one plays for 0.25 beats

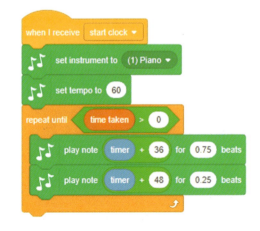

Asking questions

If you want to ask the player a question, there are two Sensing blocks you can use:

- **ask [What's your name?] and wait**: When you use this block, a box opens at the bottom of the screen for the player to type  something into, and the script the block is in pauses until the player enters something. The player can finish typing by pressing the Enter key on the keyboard, or clicking the check mark on the right of the box. The question is shown in a speech bubble and you can change it to anything you like.

- **answer**: After the player has typed something in, this block contains the answer. The information in this block is emptied when the green flag is clicked. When another question is asked, the old answer is replaced by the new answer.

When you ask a question, it looks like this:

One thing to be aware of is that if you ask a question, you'll lose the answer to your previous question, unless you've stored it in a variable. You can do that by using the **set [variable name] to 0** block, and dragging the answer block into the space where the 0 is. Variables can store text as well as numbers, so it doesn't matter what information you're saving for later. Using the blocks here, for example, you can store the player's name in the *name* variable so you can use it again later if you need to.

The "ask" block only pauses the script it is in. Other scripts continue to run, so the clock hand will keep moving while the dancer waits for the player to answer a question.

You can find the block to set the variable in the Variables section of the Blocks Palette. You need to make a variable before you can use it. To find the "ask" and "answer" blocks, click the Sensing button beside the Blocks Palette.

Joining text to greet players

When the game starts, let's ask the player their name and then say hello to them.

1 Click the dancer sprite in the Sprite List

2 Click the **Sensing** button beside the Blocks Palette and drag the **ask [What's your name?] and wait** block into the Code Area and join it to your script so far

3 Click the **Looks** button beside the Blocks Palette and add two **say Hello! for 2 seconds** blocks

4 Click the **Sensing** button beside the Blocks Palette and drag the **answer** block into the space for text in the second **say** block

5 Click the green flag to try it. When you enter your name, the dancer will say hello to you (in a speech bubble) and then say your name in another speech bubble. It would be better if we could greet the player using one speech bubble, and include their name in it

The "join apple banana" block was previously called "join hello world" in earlier versions of Scratch.

6 To do that, click the **Operators** button beside the Blocks Palette and drag in the **join apple banana** block. This block is used for joining two bits of text together. Put it into the Hello! space in your first **say** block

7 Type "Hello " (with a space after it) into the first hole in the **join** block and put an **answer** block into the other one

Above: By using the "join apple banana" operator, you can combine two bits of text in one speech bubble. Here we've combined the word "Hello", and the name the player entered.

8 Drag your second **say** block into the Blocks Palette to remove it, then click the **green flag** again. Much better!

110

Preparing the quiz

You should have a clock that's ready to tick, and a dancer who asks the player's name and greets them with a friendly hello. Now let's build the main part of the game. Add these blocks to your script for the dancer so far:

1 With timing-based games like this, it's only fair to make sure the player is ready before you start. To do this, we'll give the player a warning, with the dancer telling them "Ready, Steady, Go!". Add three **say Hello! for 2 seconds** blocks and change their message and timing

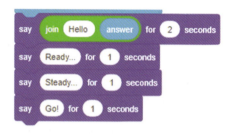

Hot tip

In the previous edition of this book, this game was started by the player pressing the spacebar. That didn't work on tablet devices, though, so I've replaced it with the "Ready, Steady, Go!" messages here. To make your games work on touch devices, avoid key sensing blocks.

2 Set the *time taken* variable to 0 and then broadcast the "start clock" message. The clock hand will start moving when it receives the "start clock" message, and it will keep going until the *time taken* variable is changed to something higher than zero

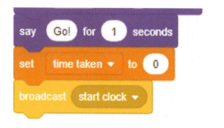

3 There are 10 questions in the quiz, so add a **repeat 10** block

111

There's a scrollbar on the right of the Code Area. Use it when you run out of room on the screen to add more blocks!

Beware

Make sure you add a space after "What is" and around the word "times", otherwise the question numbers will squash up against the words, as shown below.

Making the questions

Now you're ready to add the blocks that will create the questions:

1 Each quiz question will ask the player to multiply two numbers chosen at random. We'll put one of those numbers into the variable *number1* and the other one into the variable *number2*. Add two **set [variable name] to 0** blocks inside your **repeat** bracket. Change the variable in one to *number1*, and the other to *number2*

2 Click the **Operators** button beside the Blocks Palette and drag the **pick random 1 to 10** block into the **set number1** and **set number2** blocks. Change the second number in it to 12, so we're testing the full multiplication table

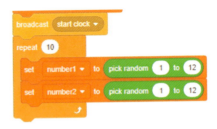

3 We're going to use the *question* variable to store our question, which will look something like "What is 5 times 9?" The actual numbers are the random numbers we put into the *number1* and *number2* variables a moment ago. We're going to build the question up using the **join apple banana** block, so start by setting the question to be "What is " (with a space at the end) joined to the variable *number1*. The **set [variable name]** block is a Variables block, and the **join apple banana** block is an Operators block

4 The next step is to add the word **"times"** (with a space either side of it) to the *question* variable.

To do this set the variable to be itself joined to the word "times"

5 Repeat that process to add *number2* to the *question* variable. Add a question mark at the end

6 Click the **Sensing** button beside the Blocks Palette and drag in **ask [What's your name?] and wait**

113

7 Click the **Variables** button and drag the variable *question* into the **ask** block

8 Click the green flag to test it! You should be asked 10 random multiplication questions. The game won't check your answers yet, though

Checking the answers

After the player enters a number, we need to check whether it is right or not. The following blocks are added underneath your blocks so far, but are still inside the bracket of the **repeat 10** block:

1 First, let's calculate the correct answer and store it in the variable *total*. Click the **Variables** button beside the Blocks Palette. Add the **set [variable name] to 0** block to your script. Set the variable name to *total*

2 Click the **Operators** button beside the Blocks Palette. Add the multiplication operator in your **set total** block

3 Click the **Variables** button beside the Blocks Palette. Drag the *number1* and *number2* variables into each side of the multiplication Operator block

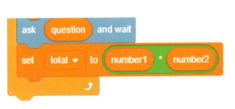

4 Click the **Control** button beside the Blocks Palette and add an **if... then... else** block

5 We want to check whether one number (the player's answer) is equal to another number (the right answer, stored in the variable *total*). Click the **Operators** button beside the Blocks Palette and drag the = block into the diamond-shaped hole in the **if...then... else** block

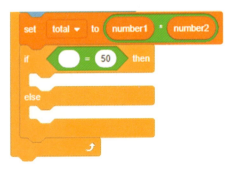

6 Click the **Sensing** button beside the Blocks Palette and drag the **answer** block into the = block

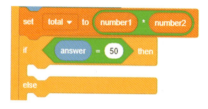

7 Click the **Variables** button beside the Blocks Palette and drag the variable *total* into the = block

8 The **if... then... else** block has two brackets. The first one contains blocks that should run if whatever we're checking for is true, so in this case, if the answer entered matches the right answer. Click the **Looks** button beside the Blocks Palette and drag a **say Hello! for 2 seconds** block into the first bracket. Change the message in it to **Correct!** and the timing to 0.5 seconds

9 Drag another **say Hello! for 2 seconds** block into the second bracket. Change the message in it to **That's not right!** and the timing to 5 seconds

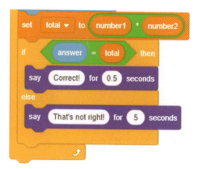

Hot tip

If the player gets it right, the game moves quickly on to the next question. If not, there's a 5-second delay before the next question, so the player suffers a time penalty.

You could adapt this game to ask more questions. Just change the number of times the main loop repeats, and the number used in calculating the average. The best approach would be to store the number of questions in a variable and drop that into your repeat block and your average calculation, so you can just change the variable value to change the number of questions.

116

Reporting the scores

Success in this game is measured by the time taken to answer the questions, the faster the better. Let's add scripts to the dancer sprite to report the scores:

1 Add the **set [variable name] to 0** block to your existing dancer script. You've finished asking your 10 questions now, so join this block underneath your **repeat 10** block, not inside it. Change the variable name to *time taken*

2 Drag the **timer** Sensing block into your **set [variable name]** block. The timer will keep on ticking, but the variable stores its value as soon as the player has answered your 10 questions. Remember that the clock hand stops moving when the *time taken* variable changes

3 Add another **set [variable name]** block to your script. Change the variable name to *average*. The average is calculated by dividing the *time taken* variable by 10, because there are 10 questions. To divide one number by another you use the / Operator block, which divides the first number by the second number

4 Add two **show variable** blocks into your script and change the variable names in them to *time taken* and *average*, to show the scores on the Stage

When you show a variable on the Stage, you can click and drag it to where you want it to be. You may find one of the variables overlaps the dancer in its default position.

Adding the victory dance

If the player answers all 10 questions quickly enough, the quizmaster does a breakdance for them:

1. Add an **if... then... else** block to your script

2. We want to check whether the average time taken is less than our target of 3 seconds, so click the **Operators** button beside the Blocks Palette and drag the < block into the diamond-shaped hole in your **if...then... else** block

3. Click the **Variables** button beside the Blocks Palette and drag the **average** block into the left of the < block. Type a number 3 into the right of it

4. Blocks inside the first bracket of the **if...then...else** block run when the average time is less than 3, so this is where we put our dance. Click the **Sound** button and

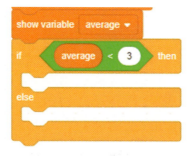

drag in the block to start the human beatbox sound effect. You'll need to choose the right sound in the block's menu

5. Add a **repeat 10** block and change the number in it to 9

The < block checks whether the number on the left is less than the number on the right.

Don't forget

Hot tip

If the average time of 3 seconds is too fast, use a bigger number instead. If you are using Scratch in the iPad's browser, you might want to increase the time because it takes longer to enter your answer using the virtual keyboard. Remember, though: If you can beat it every time, it's not challenging enough!

Hot tip

Our dance routine repeats nine times because each dance pose takes half a second and the soundtrack plays for about 4.5 seconds.

...cont'd

 Click the **Looks** button beside the Blocks Palette and drag the **next costume** block into the bracket of your **repeat** block. It changes a sprite to its next costume, and when it runs out, goes back to the first one

 Add a **wait 1 seconds** Control block, again inside your repeat bracket, and change the time in it to 0.5 seconds

8 When the dance finishes, we need to switch the dancer back to the upright costume of champ99-b. Add the **switch costume** Looks block. This belongs outside the **repeat 9** bracket (because we only want to do it once), but inside the top part of the **if...then...else** bracket (because it's still part of the victory dance). See the code below

9 Drag the **say Hello! for 2 seconds** block into the other bracket of your **if...then...else** block. This is for when the player doesn't beat the clock, so add an encouraging message to invite them to try again

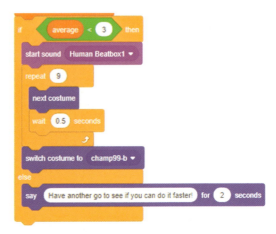

Above: Two of the dance poses from the quiz host's dance routine, celebrating a fast game.

7 Evil Robot

Create a version of the classic word game Hangman, and you'll learn how to structure more sophisticated projects using your own blocks, how to use lists to manage information, and how to write on the Stage with a sprite. You can personalize this game with your own word lists and your choice of cartoon host.

Introducing Evil Robot

In this traditional game, commonly known as Hangman, you have to guess the letters that could be in a mystery word. If you guess correctly, you're shown where your guessed letter appears in the word. If you guess wrongly, another part of the evil robot is assembled. When the robot is complete, it's game over.

This is a one-player game, with the computer randomly picking a word from a list, and telling you whether your guesses are right or wrong. The game idea might seem simple, but implementing it in Scratch will draw on most of your skills so far.

You'll learn how to:

● Make Scratch talk out loud using the Text to Speech extension, a new feature in Scratch 3.

● Store lists of information, such as lists of letters or words, and use blocks to add, find and remove items in the list.

● Write text on the Stage using a sprite with costumes for each letter of the alphabet.

● Look at individual letters in a piece of text.

● Use functions to create scripts that are easier to understand, and easier to write.

You can play this game using a tablet. I recommend using portrait orientation.

120

It's okay to experiment with your programs to see what works and what doesn't. I tried making this game another way at first, using a different sprite for each letter in the word. It was clumsy synchronizing between the sprites, so I worked out the simpler solution you'll see in this chapter.

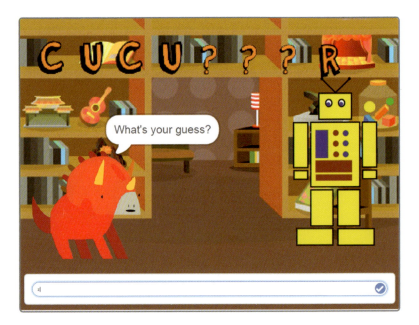

Importing the images

To start, let's create the sprite for the quiz host, and set up the backdrop you will use. The quiz host will ask you to guess a letter and tell you whether you're right or wrong. This sprite is where most of the blocks for the game will be kept.

1 We don't need the cat in this game. To delete it, click it in the Sprite List and then click the trash can icon that appears in its top-right corner

2 Add a backdrop. You'll be putting letters and the evil robot illustration on top of it, so pick something simple. I'm using the Room 1 image from the Indoors category

3 We need to add a sprite to use as the game host. I've chosen Dinosaur2 because it has some nice costumes we can use to animate the sprite while it's standing still

4 Add this script to the dinosaur sprite. It will make the sprite switch to a random costume every few seconds. The costumes show the dinosaur in different poses. It doesn't make a difference to how the game is played, but it makes the host look more interesting. I've chosen to use the first three costumes here. The fourth one shows the dinosaur rearing up, which looks less natural in this game

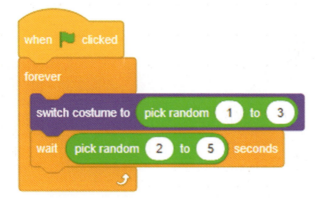

Hot tip

The "switch costume to [name]" block can be used with a costume number if you drop a variable or other number block on top of it. Evil Robot's dinosaur movement shows you how.

Hot tip

Of course, if you're writing the program, you'll know the words in it! But if you make the list long enough, you might forget the words, or you could get a friend to add some words to the program for you. In my online version of this game, I'll change the words from those used in the book so you can play the game too!

Making a block for speech

Scratch enables you to create your own blocks, and tell it what you want them to do. It's the perfect solution if you find you're reusing the same set of blocks a lot, or that your scripts are becoming extremely long.

Our Evil Robot game will feature speech, but we have to make the game playable even if players don't have speakers. Let's make a block that puts some text on the screen and says it out loud. We'll use it throughout our game.

When you make a block on a sprite, you can only use that block on the same sprite.

1 Click the **Add Extension** button in the bottom left of the Blocks Palette, and choose the Text to Speech extension. This adds the Text to Speech blocks to the Blocks Palette

2 Click the **My Blocks** button beside the Blocks Palette

3 Click the **Make a Block** button

Make a Block

4 Enter a name for your block. We'll call it "talk to player", so it's clearly different to the **say** block that Scratch has already

The Text to Speech extension is new in Scratch 3. It includes blocks to set the language (which changes the speaker's accent) and change the voice type.

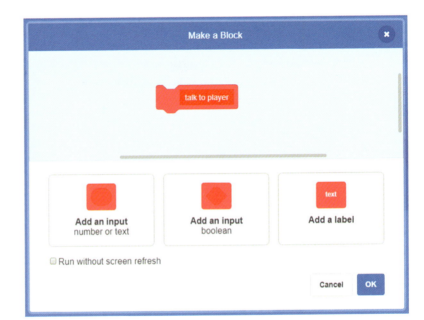

5 You can have holes in your blocks to give the block some information. Click "Add an input (number or text)"

6 Where it says "number or text", type "text to say". This is a variable that your block will use for the information you send it. You could call it anything. Click OK

Hot tip

If you make a mistake when adding an input hole in a block, click the trash can above it to remove it. To change your block later, right-click it in the Blocks Palette and choose Edit.

7 Your Code Area now has a **define** block, where you can tell Scratch what your new block should do. Add a **say** block, and a **speak** block from the Text to Speech blocks

8 The **text to say** block will store the text you send to your block. To use it in the code for your block, drag it from the **define** block, and drop it into your script

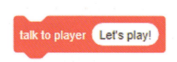

Hot tip

The purple blocks are Looks blocks. Click the Looks button beside the Blocks Palette to find them.

9 Drag your new block from the My Blocks part of the Blocks Palette to the Code Area. Type something into it and click it to test it. You should see a speech bubble on the Stage and hear the phrase spoken out loud

Making the alphabet sprite

For this game, we want to write the word guessed so far on the Stage so the player can always see their progress in the game.

To do this, we'll use a sprite with a costume for each letter of the alphabet. We'll move it to the right position, change it to the right letter, and then use the **stamp** block to leave a picture of that letter on the Stage.

As well as the letters A to Z, you need a costume with a question mark in it, which you'll use to indicate the unguessed letters in the word.

The process of making the sprite is simple, but time consuming! You can draw each letter if you prefer, but I'm going to use the letters in the sprite library.

1 Click the **Choose a Sprite** button to add a sprite from the library. Choose a letter A. There is a category for letters, but if your screen is too small to show it, you can browse all the sprites

Block-A

2 Click the **Costumes** tab

3 Click the **Choose a Costume** button to add a new costume. Choose a letter B

4 Repeat this step for the rest of the alphabet

5 There isn't a question mark sprite included in Scratch, so you'll need to paint one. I used the brush to make mine. To make the shadow, I selected my orange shape in the Paint Editor, copied it, pasted it, changed the copy's color to black, and sent it to the back. I could then drag it underneath the question mark. See Chapter 4 for a refresher on using the Paint Editor

Beware

Check you have 27 costumes, with A to Z in alphabetical order plus a question mark. This game will behave strangely if the costumes are in the wrong order.

Don't forget

If you have a set of letter images stored on your computer, remember that you can upload a costume from your computer. Hover over (or tap) the New Costume button to open the menu.

Upload Costume

Writing on the Stage

We're going to create our own block now to write on the Stage. This script works by converting the letters in a piece of text into the correct costume numbers of the alphabet sprite, so that it can be stamped on the Stage. Letter C in the game board, for example, needs to be converted into the third costume of the sprite, which shows a letter C:

1 Click your alphabet sprite in the Sprite List

2 Click the **Variables** button and make three variables called *alphabet*, *alphabet marker*, and *word marker*

3 Click **My Blocks** and make a block called "write". Give it a text input box called "text to write"

We don't need to see these variables on the Stage, so uncheck the boxes beside their blocks in the Blocks Palette.

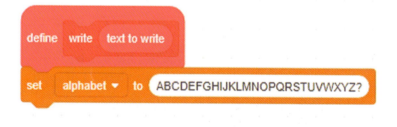

4 You'll use the existing **define** block in the Code Area to create this script. First, we'll set the *alphabet* variable to contain the alphabet plus a question mark. Check this carefully. The game won't work properly if you mistype letters here

I've written this script so you can easily reuse it. In this game, we'll store the game board as a list. We'll need to convert it to a text variable before we use this block.

5 We'll write each letter of the text in order. The variable *word marker* is used to remember which letter we've reached. We start by setting it to 1

Take care with typing the alphabet with the question mark at the end. If you get the letters in the wrong order, you'll see the wrong letters on screen when you play. A small typing error here can spoil the game.

...cont'd

Beware

Scratch sees uppercase and lowercase letters as being the same. As a result, it doesn't matter whether you guess an "E" or an "e" when playing the game.

Don't forget

The outer loop works its way through the word we're writing, one letter at a time. It uses the *word marker* variable to remember where it is. The inner loop works its way through the alphabet, one letter at a time. It uses the *alphabet marker* variable to remember where it is.

6 We need to add a **repeat 10** loop. This loop will be used to go through all the letters in the word we're writing, so replace the number in it with blocks to find the length of the word we're writing

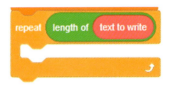

7 We'll check each character in the *alphabet* variable to see if it matches the letter from the word. The variable *alphabet marker* stores which letter we've got to. Start by setting it to 1

8 Add a **repeat until** block, inside your **repeat** block's bracket. We'll use this to keep checking the game board letter against the alphabet until we find a match. Drag an = Operator into its frame

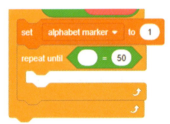

9 There is an Operator block you can use to refer to a specific letter in a piece of text called **letter 1 of apple**. Drag it in to the left of your Operator block. Replace the text "apple" with the variable *alphabet*. Replace the 1 with the variable *alphabet marker*

10 Drag in another **letter 1 of apple** block. Replace the number 1 with the variable *word marker*. Replace "apple" with the variable *text to write*

11 Add a block to increase *alphabet marker*. Because of the **repeat until** block, it keeps increasing until the letter in the alphabet is the same as the letter in the word

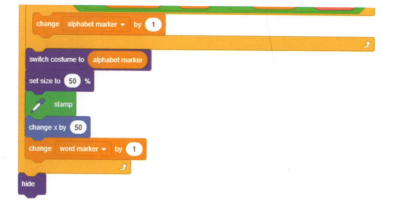

12 Now, *alphabet marker* contains the right costume number. That's because the letters and question mark in the variable *alphabet* are in the same order as the costumes. Add the Pen extension. Then add these blocks to stamp the costume on the Stage. We also advance to the next letter in the word

Don't forget

Whenever you see a "text to write" block in this script, you need to drag it from the "define" block at the top, and drop it into your script.

Beware

Take care with where you put the blocks to stamp the sprite. They should be inside your "repeat length of text to write" bracket, but outside the "repeat until" bracket.

Hot tip

Why not test your new block works? Try this short script. Add it to your alphabet sprite and click it to run it.

Designing the Evil Robot

Hot tip

You can use the line and circle drawing tools to make your robot sprite, or you can draw it freehand using the Brush tool.

1 Click the button to paint a new sprite. It's at the bottom of the Sprite List

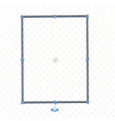

2 This first costume represents the blank page before the first line is drawn. Rename it to "empty", but don't make any other changes to it. You can find the box to rename the sprite above the canvas in the Costumes Area

3 Use the menu in the bottom left to choose to paint a new costume. Draw the torso of your robot. Start with an empty rectangle, so you can center it over the crosshairs

Don't forget

To add a new costume to your sprite, click the Choose a Costume button in the bottom left of the Costumes Area.

4 Draw your robot. You can copy my picture, or make up your own. It needs to have 11 different elements in it (see facing page)

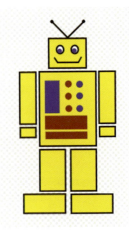

5 In the sprite's Costumes Area, right-click on the costume and then select **duplicate**. Repeat this process until you have 13 costumes in total: one blank, and 12 robots

6 Go into your costumes and delete the parts you don't need in each one. After the empty costume, the first one shows one foot, the second one another foot, the third one a leg, and so on. See how the sequence looks below. (Costumes 12 and 13 should both have complete robots)

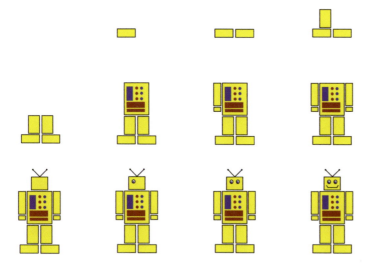

7 The final costume is there for you to add animation. When you lose the game and the robot attacks, the script will switch between costumes 12 and 13. Add some small changes to the last costume. I've added electrical charge between the antennas, changed the button colors and made the eyes glow red. You could make the arms and legs move if you wanted to

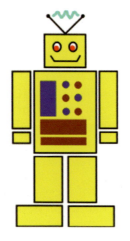

Hot tip

You can uncheck the boxes beside all the variables and lists in this project. It's usually a good idea to uncheck variables as you make them, unless you know you're going to need to see their values on the Stage.

Creating the variables

We're going to need some more variables in this game.

Click the **Variables** button beside the Blocks Palette and then click the **Make a Variable** button to make the following variables. Some variables are needed only by one sprite (*score* is only used by the quiz host, and *word marker* is only used by the letter sprite), but others are needed by all sprites. To avoid the complexity of clicking between the sprites to set up different variables for them, set up all the variables to work on all sprites:

- *game board variable*: This is used to write on the Stage.

- *game over status*: This variable stores the value PLAYING, LOST or WON, depending on the game.

- *letter number*: This variable will be used as a counter when preparing the game board for display on the Stage.

- *letter number guessed*: This variable stores the position in the word where the player has made a correct guess. For example, if they guess "s" in the word "desk", the variable stores 3.

- *score*: This records how many letters the player has correctly guessed. When it matches the word length, they've won.

- *word length*: This variable stores the length of the word the player is trying to guess. When the player's score matches the word length, they've won. We could write our program without the variable *word length*, and just use the **length of apple** Operator block each time we need to know the length of the word. That takes two blocks, though, so it's slower to write and having one block is easier to read.

- *word to guess*: This is the word the player is trying to figure out. It will be randomly chosen at the start of the game.

alphabet

alphabet marker

game board variable

game over status

letter number

letter number guessed

my variable

score

word length

word marker

word to guess

Using loop counters

When you're using a loop to repeat, it's sometimes useful to know how many times you've been around the loop. For example, here's a script that counts to 10. It can only do this if it remembers which number it's got to, and increases it each time it repeats.

You can use this script as a template whenever you need to create a loop that counts.

You've already seen the *alphabet marker* variable being used when writing on the Stage. It counts through the alphabet until it reaches the right letter. The *word marker* variable counts through each letter in the word that's being written too. We'll make a script later on that uses *letter number* as a counter to show the game board.

Hot tip

You can try building this counting script. Just click it to run it. What if you wanted it to count from 5 to 25? Then you'd set the starting value in the first block to 5, and change the "repeat 10" block to repeat 20 times.

131

Hiding variables on the Stage

When you add a variable, it's shown on the Stage. Uncheck the boxes beside the variable names in the Blocks Palette to hide them again. With so many variables, the Stage will be half-covered with them otherwise. One of those variables will contain the answer the player is trying to guess, too, which would make the game rather pointless.

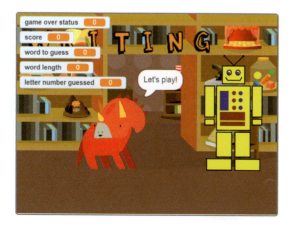

Animating the robot

Let's add the animation scripts to the robot.

1 The robot plays the sounds when the game ends. Click the **Sounds** tab and add "Trap Beat" and "Dance Around" from the Loops category of the sounds library

2 When the game begins, we want to put the robot in the right place and reset its costume. Add this script

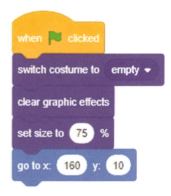

3 Drag a **when I receive [message]** block into the Code Area. Click the menu in the block to create a new message called "wrong guess". Use it as the starting point for the script below

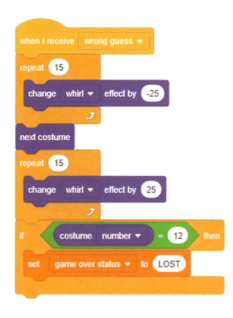

4 Add this script to your robot. You'll need to create a new broadcast

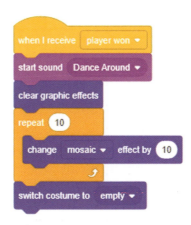

The "player lost" sequence shows how you can create a simple movement animation, with the sprite changing costumes each step. You can use a costume name or a block containing a costume number in the "switch costume" block.

5 Now add this script. Again, you need to make a new broadcast to start it

Below: The "wrong guess" sequence uses the whirl effect. The robot turns in on itself, adds a piece and then unfolds to show the new piece.

6 Click the **green flag**. Now, click the "wrong guess" script repeatedly to see the robot assemble itself. Click the "player won" sequence to test it. Repeat this process (from the green flag), but this time try the "player lost" sequence

Adding the main game code

Let's add the main game script to the dinosaur sprite.

1 Click the dinosaur sprite in the Sprite List

2 Click the **My Blocks** button beside the Blocks Palette. Make new blocks called "set up variables", "create game board", "get player's guess", "check the letter", and "game over sequence"

You can read this script to see how the game will work. It will set up the variables, make the game board and display it, announce the start of the game, and then keep asking for guesses and checking them until the game is won or lost. The beauty of making our own blocks is that it makes scripts easier to read, and shorter too. Imagine the complexity if the instructions for all these blocks were in one long script.

3 Add the script shown below to the dinosaur sprite. You'll need to use the menu in the broadcast block to create a new message called "show board". Make sure you drag in the **broadcast [message] and wait** block, and not the similar **broadcast [message]** block

4 You can click the green flag to position your dinosaur and hear its opening words. The game won't do anything else yet, because we have more scripts to add

Take care adding the "=" blocks. Wait until the space in the "or" block is glowing before releasing the mouse button, otherwise your "=" block might replace the "or" block instead of going inside it.

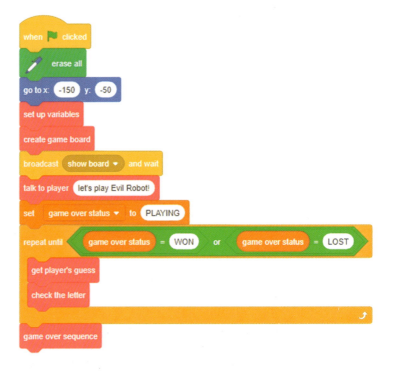

Creating lists

As well as variables, Scratch gives you another way to store information, which is in a list. A list is perfect for organizing similar items, such as numbers in a high-score table or words in a quiz game. We'll use three lists in Evil Robot: one for the pool of words that the mystery word is taken from, one for the game board, and one to remember the letters the player has guessed so we can stop them guessing the same letter twice.

To create a list, follow these steps:

1 Click the **Variables** button beside the Blocks Palette

2 Click the **Make a List** button. A box opens, like the one used to make a variable

3 Enter the name for the list in the box. We'll need a list called *game board*, so enter this name now. The *game board* list will be used for the mystery word as seen by the player, a mixture of guessed letters and question marks for unguessed ones

4 As with variables, you can make a list for all sprites or just for one sprite. Check that this list will be available to all sprites

5 Repeat these steps to make a new list, this time called *word list*. Add more lists called *word to guess list* and *guessed letters*

6 As with a variable, lists are displayed on the Stage when they're created. They take up much more room, though. Uncheck the box beside each list name in the Blocks Palette to hide it from the Stage. Remember you can check it again if you want to see what's going on in the list, though – for example, if you need to debug a script

Hot tip

To delete a list or variable, right-click its name in the Blocks Palette and then click Delete in the menu. Be warned that if you delete a variable or list, any blocks still using it are also deleted from your scripts.

Lists aren't reset when a program ends. If you run a program that adds things to a list, each time it runs the list gets longer, joining on to where it finished last time around.

Hot tip

For a short demo of lists, see Penguin Patter in Chapter 10.

Using lists

When you make a list in Scratch, it adds blocks to the Variables part of the Blocks Palette for managing them. The new blocks are:

- **add thing to [list name]**: This block adds something to the end of your list. You can type a word or number where it says "thing", or you can drag in a variable or a rounded block like the **x position** or **timer**. With all these blocks, use the menu in the block to choose which list you want to use.

- **delete 1 of [list name]**: This block is used to remove an item. Any items after the deleted item move up the list so there's no gap. If you repeatedly delete the first item, the whole list eventually disappears. You can use other numbers here (2 for the second item, and so on).

- **delete all of [list name]**: This empties your list completely.

- **insert thing at 1 of [list name]**: Use this to insert an item in the list. Any items after the inserted item shuffle further down the list to make room. You can change "thing" to different text, a number or a rounded block, such as a variable. You can type another position number or use a variable in place of the 1.

- **replace item 1 of [list name] with thing**: Use this to replace an item in the list with another. You can edit the number to choose a different list item, and can change "thing" to alternative text, a number, or a rounded block.

- **item 1 of [list name]**: This rounded block is used to get information out of your list again. You could drag it into a **say** block, for example, or set a variable using it. You can change the number or replace it with a variable.

- **item # of thing in [list name]**: This will tell you where an item (such as the word "thing") is in your list. If it's in there more than once, it gives you the lowest number position.

- **length of [list name]**: This block is like a variable that always tells you how many items are in the list.

- **[list name] contains thing**: Use this block to see whether "thing", or the text or number you use in the block, is in the list. The block is shaped like a diamond, and you'll most often put it inside an **if** block's frame to make a decision based on whether something's in a list or not. When you add a variable to a list, you actually add the variable's contents. The list doesn't remember which variable the contents came from. Imagine there's a variable called *name* and one called *winner*, and they both have the same text in them. If you add *name* to the list, and then check whether the list contains *winner*, the answer will be yes.

- **show list [list name]**: This block will show your list on the Stage, as you can see on the right. When there are too many list items to fit in the box, there is a scrollbar to see more. You can click and drag the bottom-right corner of the list box to make it bigger or smaller. The plus button in the bottom left is used to add a new list item. You can also click the list items in this box and edit them.

- **hide list [list name]**: This block hides your list on the Stage.

The "item # of thing in [list name]" is a new block in Scratch 3. It makes it much easier to search lists.

Before you can use these blocks with a list, you must click the Make a List button to create the list.

You can type or import data into a list using the list's box when it's displayed on the Stage. Click the + to type in an entry. Right-click the box to choose to import or export list data.

Don't forget

If we didn't delete the lists at the start of the game, they would get longer every time someone played, and the game would behave strangely.

138

Hot tip

You can test this script. In the Variables part of the Blocks Palette, check the box beside the variable *word to guess*, so you can see what it contains on the Stage. Click this new script to run it. You should see it pick a random word from your list and put it into this variable. Try it a few times. Words will often repeat, unless you have a huge list.

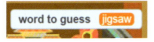

word to guess | jigsaw

Setting up the variables

Now we'll define the set up variables block. Follow these steps:

1 Click the dinosaur sprite in the Sprite List

2 Find the **define set up variables** block in your Code Area

3 Click the **Variables** button and add two blocks to delete all of the *guessed letters* and *word list* lists

4 Add a **set score to 0** block

5 Add some words to your word list. Your script so far is shown on the right

6 Add on a **set [variable name] to 0** block. Change the variable to *word to guess*

7 Drop the **item 1 of [list name]** block into the **set word to guess** block's hole. Set the list name in the new block to *word list*

8 Click the **Operators** button and drag in a **pick random 1 to 10** block. Click the **Variables** button, and drag a **length of [variable name]** block into the second hole. Change the list name in this block to be *word list* too

9 Add the final blocks to set up the *word length* variable

Creating the game board

The *game board* list stores the word as the player sees it in the game. Each list item is one character. At first, the list is full of question marks. As the player guesses letters, the correct letters replace the question marks. I chose a list for this, instead of a variable, because there is a block we can use to easily replace a letter in a list.

The game also uses a list called *word to guess* list. This stores the word the player must guess, with each list item being one letter. I set up this list because the **item # of thing in [list name]** block makes it easy to search the list for the letter the player guessed.

1 On the dinosaur sprite, find the **define create game board** block. Add two blocks to empty **word to guess list** and the **game board** list

2 We'll use a repeat loop to go through each letter of the word the player must guess, and add it to *word to guess list*. The variable *letter number* is used to count our position in the word. The repeating code is wrapped in a **repeat 10** block, with the 10 replaced with the length of the word. The loop also adds a question mark to the *game board* list for each letter in the word

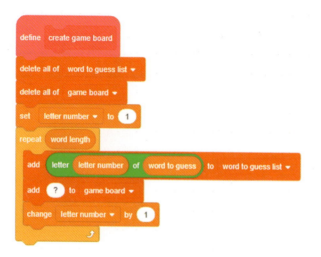

The Operator block "letter 1 of apple" picks a letter out of a piece of text. In this script, we use it to take each letter from our mystery word and add it to "word to guess list", so we replace the number 1 with the variable *letter number*.

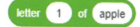

In the Variables part of the Blocks Palette, check the box beside the two lists so you can see them on the Stage. Click this new script to run it. The game board should contain question marks. The word to guess should be a word broken down into letters.

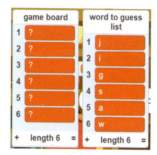

139

Showing the game board

At the start of the game, the quiz host sends a broadcast called "show board". A script on the alphabet sprite will respond to that, and write the game board onto the Stage. It'll use the block you already created to write using a sprite. Because the game board is stored as a list, and the script to write on the Stage uses a variable, it needs to convert the game board from a list to a variable first.

1 Click the alphabet sprite in the Sprite List

2 Add this script (right). In the last block, delete the 0 in the hole and leave it empty. We need an empty *game board* variable to begin with

3 Add the script below at the end of your script so far. Use a **repeat 10** block and drop the **length of game board** block on top. The script joins the letters from the game board list to the game board variable, one at a time. At the end, it writes the *game board* variable on the Stage. For now, it's all question marks. Later on, this will show a mix of question marks and guessed letters

Below: The Stage with question marks representing letters in the mystery word.

4 Click the green flag. You should see a sequence of question marks appear on the Stage

Asking for the player's guess

Let's add some interaction with the player now!

1   Click the dinosaur in the Sprite List

2   Find the **define get player's guess** block in the Code Area

3   We should keep asking until the player enters a single letter they haven't used before. Add a **repeat until** block from the Control part of the Blocks Palette and an **and** Operator block

4   Drag an = block into the holes in the **and** block

5   Drag the **length of apple** Operator block into one of the = blocks and drag the **answer** Sensing block onto that. Change the other side of the = operator to 1

6   Drag an **item # of thing in [list name]** block into the other = block. Drag the **answer** block onto that and change the list to *guessed letters*. Change the other side of the = operator to 0. Now this script will repeat until the answer contains a single character that isn't in the *guessed letters* list

Hot tip

The "item # of thing in [list name]" block gives you 0 if the item isn't in the list.

Hot tip

We can also use a "not" block and a "[list name] contains thing" block to check whether something is not in a list.

Hot tip

It's a good idea to make sure the player enters something sensible. This is called validating the input. In this game, we check that they enter a single character that isn't in the list of previous letters. We could go further by confirming their input is a letter, and not a number, for example.

...cont'd

Don't forget

When you use an "ask" block, the "answer" block stores what the player types in. At the start of the game it's empty.

answer

Don't forget

Take care with your brackets. The "if" bracket and everything inside it goes inside your "repeat until" bracket, otherwise the player wouldn't be asked to guess again when they guessed the same letter.

Hot tip

Click the green flag to test the game so far. When you enter the same letter twice, the game should tell you.

 7 Inside this loop, ask the player to guess a letter

8 Players find it hard to remember which letters they've already guessed, so we should check for them. The list *guessed letters* remembers their previous guesses. Drag an **if** block into your **repeat until** bracket. Drag the **[list name] contains thing** block into the **if** block's frame, click the menu in it to choose the list *guessed letters*, and add the **answer** block in place of "thing". Inside this **if** bracket, tell the player they've already guessed the letter

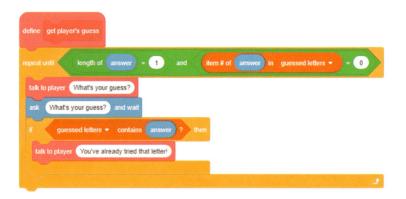

9 The **repeat until** loop ends when the player has entered a single letter that isn't in the list of previously guessed letters. To finish this script, we should add their guess to the list of guessed letters for checking on future goes

Checking the letter

The next scripts we will add to our main sprite check whether the player's guess is in the word. If it is, it's added to the game board and that's updated on screen. If not, the robot grows bigger:

 1   Click the dinosaur in the Sprite List

2   Find the **define check the letter** block in the Code Area. Click the **Control** button and add in an **if...then...else** block. We'll use this to check whether the guess was right, and do one thing if it was, and something else if it wasn't

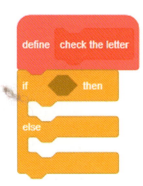

3   The **apple contains a?** block is used to check whether a piece of text contains another piece of text. Drag it into the diamond hole on your **if...then...else** block. Add the **word to guess** variable block on one side. Drag an **answer** block into the other side

4   Go to the My Blocks part of the Blocks Palette and click Make a Block. Create a new block called "process correct guess". It doesn't need to have any input holes in it

The new "apple contains a?" Operator block can be used to search a variable or a list for a piece of text. You can search for whole words, not just one letter. This block only tells you whether it's there, though, and not what position it's at. That's why I used the "item # of thing in [list name]" to find letter positions in this game.

...cont'd

Don't forget

Creating blocks to organize our scripts, and using meaningful names for both the blocks and variables, makes it easy to see what a program will do.

Don't forget

All the list-related blocks are in the Variables part of the Blocks Palette. You might need to scroll down to see them.

5 If the player guessed correctly, we'll congratulate them with a message and run the **process correct guess** block, which we'll make next. If not, we'll broadcast the message "wrong guess". The robot sprite will receive this and use it to start its script that makes it assemble another part. Add the blocks as shown here:

```
define  check the letter

if  ( word to guess  contains  answer  ? )  then

    process correct guess

    talk to player  Correct guess!

else

    broadcast  wrong guess ▼  and wait

    talk to player  Sorry! That letter isn't in the word.
```

6 You can now click the **green flag** to test your game so far. Check the box beside the *word to guess* variable in the Variables part of the Blocks Palette. It will show you the word on the Stage. Now you can test guessing correct and incorrect letters. You should see an appropriate message. If you guess wrongly, the robot will start to appear

7 The "process correct guess" script runs when the player has guessed correctly. It needs to find out where in the word the guessed letter occurs. It might be there more than once. Start by finding the **define process correct guess** block in the Code Area, and joining a **repeat until** block to it

8 We'll use *word to guess list* to see whether the letter is in the word. When we find it, we'll remove it from that list, and add it in the same position in the game board. We want to keep checking for letters until there are no matching letters left in *word to guess list*. Add an = block, change the number to 0, and add an **item # of thing in [list name]** block. Replace "thing" with an **answer** block, and change the list to *word to guess list*

Hot tip

I replaced the letter in the "word to guess list" with three stars so it stands out. We could have used any non-letter character or sequence here.

9 We set the *letter number guessed* variable to be the position of the guessed letter in the word. We replace that position in *word to guess list* with *** and fill that position in the game board with the answer. For each correct guess, we increase the score. This loop repeats until there aren't any more of the guessed letters in the word. Add the new blocks shown below in your **repeat until** bracket

NEW

This script shows how powerful the "item # of thing in [list name]" block is. It's giving us the position of an item in the list in a single block. This block is new in Scratch 3 and the first edition of this book had to use a complicated script to do this job in earlier versions of Scratch.

...cont'd

10 Now we've updated the game board, let's display it. Add a **broadcast show board and wait** block underneath your **repeat until** block

11 After we've finished checking for correct letters in the word, we need to check whether the player has completed the word. Add these blocks underneath your **broadcast and wait** block

12 The final script we need to add to the dino is the game over sequence. Use the **define game over sequence** block in the Code Area to start it, and drag in an **if...then...else** Control block. The two broadcasts here tell the robot to do one of its Game Over animations: it either closes in on the quiz host menacingly, or explodes

13 Test the game by trying right and wrong guesses, entering repeated letters, and playing the game to completion, both winning and losing

8 Space Swarm

Use what you've learned so far and build on it to make an arcade game. You'll learn how to use loops to create special effects, how to enable a sprite to fire at another sprite, and how to make a high score table.

Beware

This game requires keyboard controls, so you can't play it on tablet devices.

Introducing Space Swarm

We're under attack! As the aliens swarm around the planet, eager to plunder all of its resources, only one person can save us. You!

Space Swarm, in the spirit of classic arcade games, sees you firing on enemies and dodging their invasion. The aliens rush in towards you from the right of the screen, zig-zagging in random directions. To play the game, move your character with the arrow keys and press the spacebar to fire. You lose one of your three lives each time an alien hits you.

This game brings together much of what you've learned in previous chapters, and will also show you how to:

- Add special effects to make sprites materialize and evaporate.

- Enable one sprite to fire upon another.

- Use flags to swap information between sprites.

- Add looping music to your game.

- Make a high score table that remembers the best score anyone has achieved playing your game on the Scratch website.

- Give the player three lives.

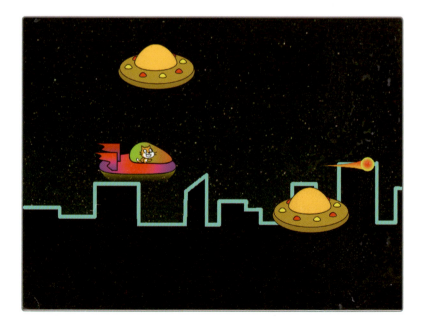

Creating the images

Let's make the player, alien, missile and other images.

1 Choose to paint a new sprite. Use the Circle tool to draw a circle. This will be the cockpit for the flying saucer

2 Select the Reshape tool. Use the handles to flatten the bottom and sharpen the top a little. You can use the Select tool to stretch the shape or change its size

3 Draw another ellipse underneath it for the base of the saucer. Use the **Backward** button to send it behind the cockpit. Adjust its position, size and shape using the Select tool until it looks right

4 Select that base ellipse using the Select tool. Click Copy above the canvas, and then click Paste. Change the fill color of the duplicate to make it a bit darker. Adjust its size and position so it forms the underside of the saucer

5 Select the cockpit and duplicate that. We'll use it as a light around the rim of the saucer, so use the Select tool to reduce its size. Color it yellow, and duplicate it several times. Arrange it around your saucer. Change alternate lights to be red

6 In the left of the Costumes Area, right-click your new costume and choose Duplicate. In the duplicated costume, swap the colors of the lights, so red becomes yellow and yellow becomes red

Use the layer buttons above the canvas to arrange which shapes appear in front. I've put two lights half-behind the dome so it looks like they go all the way around.

Forward   Backward   Front   Back

149

You can use the pipette tool to grab the light colors from the canvas to get an exact match. Open the Fill color box and select the pipette in the bottom right of it.

...cont'd

Hot tip

You can use the graduated fill options to make one color fade into another. I faded red into yellow to make a fireball.

7 Create your player sprite, facing right. I used a similar technique to the flying saucer. To make the fins, I added a square and reshaped it. First I made a top-heavy fin with a straight edge. Then I added reshaping points and used them to add the curves. I added a shape with a gradient fill that goes from yellow to transparent ink, to make it look like light shining underneath. I copied the cat costume from the cat sprite, erased its legs, and dropped it in the pilot's seat

8 Create a sprite to use as your missile. It should be designed as if firing towards the right. Mine looks like a fireball

9 Create a sprite to use as your Game Over message. I copied my text and added two layers of it in shadow: one dark green, and one black so it stands out on top of other sprites

10 Rename your player's sprite to "ship", your missile sprite to "missile", and your alien to "alien" (see page 66 in Chapter 4)

11 Import the Stars backdrop (find it in the Space category). Click the Stage beside the Sprite List and then click the **Backdrops** tab to find the Paint Editor. Draw a futuristic skyline and use the Brush to remove stars below buildings

Adding sound effects

As you learned in Chapter 5, a sprite can only play sound effects that have been added to it. This game has a techno beat to keep the blood pumping, a scream when the player is hit, a mournful trumpet when the game ends, and some alien noises too:

1 Click the ship sprite in the Sprite List

2 Click the **Sounds** tab, and click the button to choose a sound from the library. It's in the bottom left

3 Add the sound Techno from the Loops category. Repeat these steps to add the sound Scream2 from the Voice category

4 Click the alien in the Sprite List and add the Spiral sound effect. It is in the Space category

5 Add the Laser1 sound to your missile sprite. You can find it, and any other effects, using the search box at the top of the sounds library

6 The sprite with the Game Over message needs three sounds: Trumpet1, Trumpet2 and Triumph. The trumpet sounds are in the Notes category, and Triumph is among the Loops

Hot tip

To tidy up, delete the cat sprite. You won't be using it in this game, so you can get rid of it.

Don't forget

Refer back to Chapter 5 for detailed advice on adding sound effects to a sprite if you need help.

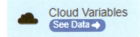

Cloud Variables
See Data ➡

Creating the variables

In this game, we're going to use Cloud variables for the first time. They enable information from your project to be saved centrally on the Scratch computers, and then accessed by other people who use your project. Space Swarm uses the Cloud variable *high score* to remember the highest score that anyone has ever achieved in the game.

You create Cloud variables in the same way you make ordinary variables, by clicking the **Variables** button, and then clicking the **Make a Variable** button in the Blocks Palette. Enter your variable name, check the box beside "Cloud variable", and click **OK**. Cloud variables are always available for all sprites. After you've made one, you can identify it because it has a fluffy cloud symbol in its block (see *high score* variable image above).

We'll use three variables in this program:

● *score*: This variable will keep track of the score in the current game. In this game, the player and alien sprites will use it, so create it for all sprites.

● *player hit*: We'll use this variable to remember whether the player has been hit or not, by storing the word "YES" or "NO" in it. When there are lots of scripts working at the same time, a variable like this can be used to keep track of the state of the game. In this game, we'll use this variable to stop the player from moving or firing after they've been hit. Create this variable and make it work for all sprites. Variables that are used like this to remember the state of part of the game are sometimes called flags.

● *high score*: Create this variable and check the box to make it a Cloud variable. If lots of people play your game, or one person replays it, this cloud variable will be used to remember the highest score across all those games.

Programming the hero

Now the variables have been set up, we can start to build the scripts for our hero character, which the player will control:

1 Click your ship sprite in the Sprite List. Drag in a Variable block to reset *score* to zero. The player and aliens can use the full Stage area, so hide the *score* and *high score* variables to stop them getting in the way

2 We're going to assemble blocks next that make the player appear, give the player control until they die, and then show what happens when they're hit. To give the player three lives, we'll do all of this three times. Drag a **repeat 10** Control block into your script, and change the number to 3

3 The variable *player hit* is used to remember whether the player has been hit or not. At the start of each life, we set it to NO

4 Add the blocks to set up the sprite's appearance, including moving it to the front (so it appears on top of all other sprites), clearing graphic effects, and putting it in its starting position (x:-165, y:0) and direction (90, facing right). For my sprite, I set the size to 50%

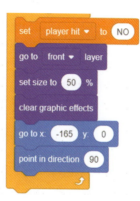

...cont'd

Below: The last half of the teleport sequence. This happens rapidly, so players will just see blobs of color coming together to make the ship appear in space.

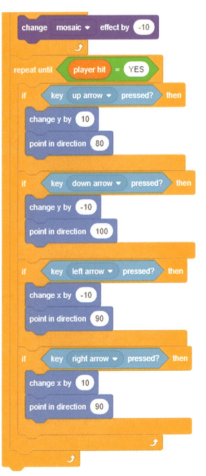

5 We'll make the sprite teleport in by using the mosaic effect. Starting it high and reducing it to zero makes the sprite materialize as if it's arrived in pieces and then morphed together

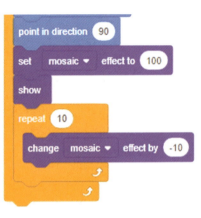

```
point in direction 90
set mosaic ▼ effect to 100
show
repeat 10
    change mosaic ▼ effect by -10
```

6 Add a **repeat until** Control block underneath the teleporter's repeat 10 block. Add the = Operator block into its frame. Drag the *player hit* variable into one side, and type YES into the other side. We'll use this loop to enable the player to move until they're hit

7 Add the blocks to control the sprite inside the bracket of the **repeat until** block. These are similar to the controls you used for Super Dodgeball

```
change mosaic ▼ effect by -10

repeat until  player hit = YES
    if  key up arrow ▼ pressed?  then
        change y by 10
        point in direction 80
    if  key down arrow ▼ pressed?  then
        change y by -10
        point in direction 100
    if  key left arrow ▼ pressed?  then
        change x by -10
        point in direction 90
    if  key right arrow ▼ pressed?  then
        change x by 10
        point in direction 90
```

8 When the **repeat until** loop ends, the player has died. The sequence for losing a life makes the ship spin in a circle and fade away using the ghost effect. The Scream2 sound gives an audible yelp. Put these blocks outside the **repeat until** bracket, but inside your **repeat 3** bracket

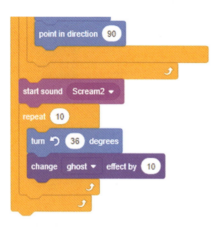

Below: The ship tilts when you move up or down. Click the green flag to try it now!

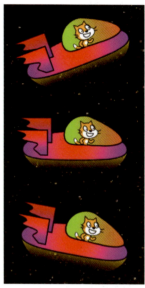

9 Finally, hide the sprite and add a short delay before the next life begins. Send a broadcast "cloak alien", which hides the aliens so they can't hit the player while the ship is materializing. These blocks go inside your **repeat 3** bracket, but outside any other brackets

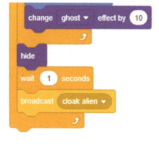

Hot tip

I added a script to my backdrop so that when the green flag is clicked, the color effect is set to a random number between 1 and 200. That makes the skyline look a different color each time the game is played.

10 When the **repeat 3** loop ends, the player has died three times, so it's game over. Create a broadcast called "game over" to alert all the other sprites. This block joins underneath your **repeat 3**

Enabling the player to fire

Let's set up the missile to fire now.

1 Click the missile in the Sprite List

2 Add this script to your sprite, to hide the missile when the game starts, and position it behind the ship

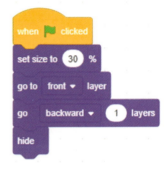

3 Click **My Blocks** beside the Blocks Palette and click **Make a Block**. Call your block "fire missile"

4 Add a script to the sprite that continuously checks for the spacebar being pressed, and then runs the **fire missile** block when it is

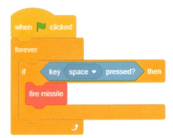

5 Add the script for the "fire missile" block. We don't want to fire when the player has been hit, so we wrap everything in an **if** block that checks for this. The script moves the sprite to the ship's position, and the loop moves the missile right until it's off screen

6 Click that last script to see (and hear!) the missile fire

Hot tip

Using 20 steps for the missile movement makes it faster than anything else in the game.

Hot tip

Only one missile can be fired at a time. This is because all of the "fire missile" script runs before the project checks the spacebar again.

Moving and shooting aliens

The alien uses the pixelate effect to materialize in a random position on the right. It makes a zig-zag pattern across the Stage by pointing in a random left-facing direction, making 8 movements, and then changing direction, until it

reaches the left of the Stage. The picture shows paths in different colors, drawn with the pen.

You can have several scripts on the same sprite, and you can use the green flag to start all of them.

1 Click the alien in the Sprite List

2 Add the script shown below to your alien sprite. The pixelate effect is used to fade it into view, and the **forever** loop keeps it moving all the time, even when it's hidden

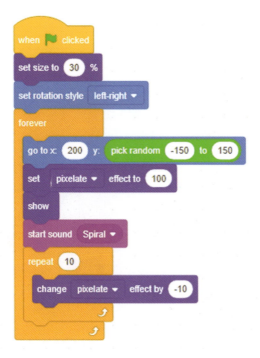

Adjust the size of the sprite in this script as appropriate for your sprite design. Smaller aliens make it easier for the player to avoid hitting them, but make it harder for the missile to hit them too.

...cont'd

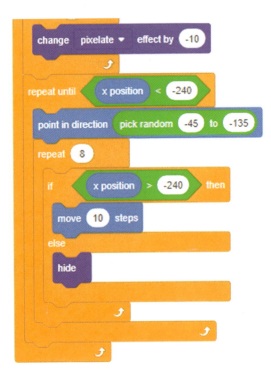

Above: Arrows indicate the range of directions the sprite can choose. The upper arrow shows direction -45, and the lower one shows -135. The alien can randomly pick any direction between them to move left across the Stage.

3 Add the movement script underneath your pixelating loop. The new script points in a random direction, then moves 8 times. It repeats this until the sprite is off the Stage. During our **repeat 8** loop, we need to check if the sprite goes off Stage and hide it if so. The random direction means we don't know when the alien will reach the edge. This script goes inside your **forever** bracket

```
change  pixelate ▼  effect by  -10

repeat until  x position  <  -240
    point in direction  pick random  -45  to  -135
    repeat  8
        if  x position  >  -240  then
            move  10  steps
        else
            hide
```

4 Add this separate script to hide the sprite while the player is materializing. The alien continues to cross the screen unseen and reappears when it rematerializes at the right

```
when I receive  cloak alien ▼
hide
```

5 The final alien script detects when the alien touches the ship or missile. When the player is hit, the variable *player hit* is set to YES. When the alien touches the missile (which means the alien's been shot), the *score* increases, the alien is shrunk, and a loop changes its color effect. It looks like the alien drifts away in space while glowing hot. The sprite is hidden and its size reset, and it is moved off the left of the screen. That makes the movement loop in the other alien script end, so the alien regenerates again on the right

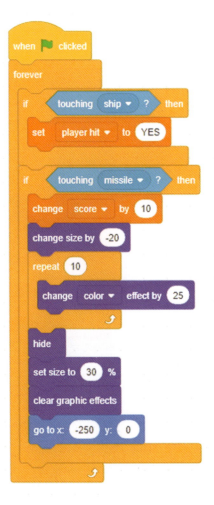

We use the variable to store whether the player's been hit, instead of using a broadcast to tell the other sprites, because a broadcast is used to start a new script running. Instead, we need to change how the existing scripts behave, especially the ship script that gives us three lives.

Finishing touches

Now add the final touches to your game!

1 Add this script to your alien sprite to animate it. When I put the **next costume** block inside the movement loop, it looked flickery, so I've put it in a separate script with a delay to slow it down

2 Right-click the alien sprite in the Sprite List and duplicate it. Now you have two aliens to contend with!

3 Add this script to your ship sprite to play music throughout the game. The **if** block stops the tune from starting again during the Game Over sequence

Hot tip

Try customizing the game. You could give each alien a different movement pattern and design, or make one faster than the other (change the number of steps it moves).

4 Click the Game Over sprite and add a script to hide the message when the game begins

5 Add this script to the Game Over sprite to play the trumpet, zoom the sprite in by increasing its size, play the second trumpet and then show the variable *score*

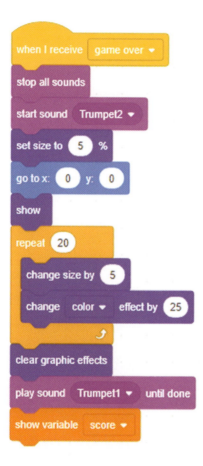

Hot tip

If the aliens are too fast, change the number in their "move 10 steps" blocks to something smaller.

161

6 Finally, use the **stop all** block to stop all scripts on all sprites

Above: The final Game Over screen, with one alien still shown.

There is a "username" Sensing block. This tells you the player's username on the Scratch website. You can use it to greet or congratulate players who use your games with a script like the one below.

The *high score* variable is stored on the Scratch computers, and is shared by everyone who plays the game on the website. You can tell it's a Cloud variable, because it has a cloud picture beside its name in the variable blocks.

Adding the high score

One way to keep players coming back for more is to challenge them to be the best ever at the game. We'll keep a record of the highest score achieved (by any players playing the game on the Scratch website), and play a triumphant tune if the player beats the record. This feature only works when using Scratch online.

Add this script immediately before the **stop all** block in your Game Over script:

1 The best ever score is stored in the Cloud variable *high score*. Drag in **show variable high score**

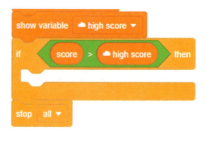

2 Drag in an **if** Control block. We're going to see whether one number is higher than another, so drag the > Operator block into its frame

3 Drag the *score* variable into the left of the > block, and the *high score* variable into the right of it

4 Inside the **if** bracket, put the blocks we want to run if this is a new high score. These blocks update *high score* to the player's *score*, and then play some triumphant music to celebrate!

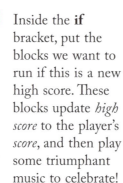

9 Physical Computing with Scratch

Design new ways to interact with Scratch using hardware devices such as webcams, microphones, the Sense HAT add-on for the Raspberry Pi, and the micro:bit. This chapter includes two games that use tilt sensors and instructions for controlling a light connected to a Raspberry Pi. You'll also see how to make a clap-o-meter and games that respond to your actions on camera.

The new extensions feature in Scratch 3 has been used to add support for the Sense HAT and the micro:bit.

Check out our companion titles, Raspberry Pi in easy steps, Raspberry Pi 3 in easy steps, and Electronics in easy steps at www.ineasysteps. com, for more information on these topics.

What is physical computing?

Physical computing is all about building computer projects that interact with the real world. In this chapter, we'll explore how different sensors can be used to control Scratch projects. We'll also introduce the simple electronics extension for the Raspberry Pi.

You'll see:

- How Scratch can detect motion on a webcam, and how you can use that to control action on the Stage.

- How Scratch can detect volume using a microphone connected to your computer, and use that to control scripts. We'll make a clap-o-meter, as used on TV talent shows to measure which act gets most audience applause.

- How the Sense HAT add-on for the Raspberry Pi can be used to detect movement, and to display messages using an 8x8 grid of multicolored lights. We'll make a game where you tilt the device to move around the screen, and use the tiny joystick to fire in four directions.

- How the micro:bit device can be used to detect movement and button pushes. We'll make a game that demands physical precision as you tilt the device to control a floating balloon.

- How to connect up an LED to the Raspberry Pi and turn it on and off using the simple electronics extension.

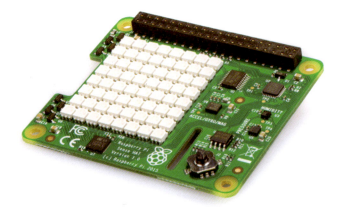

Right: The Sense HAT adds sensors to a Raspberry Pi computer. In this chapter, you'll see how to use it as a game controller.

Using a webcam

Click the **Add Extension** button in the bottom left of the Blocks Palette to add the Video Sensing blocks.

The four Video Sensing blocks are:

- **turn video on**: Use this block to turn the video off or on. It is turned on automatically for you when you add the Video Sensing extension. The video looks like a mirror, so writing is reversed. There's an option in this block to turn the video on flipped, which fixes that.

- **set video transparency to 50%**: The video appears on top of the Stage, and you can decide how much

of the backdrop you want to show through. Change the percentage to 0 to see only the video with no backdrop, and change it to 100 to see just the backdrop, without any video. When using video to control a sprite, the user will need to see themselves on screen, so 50 is often ideal.

- **video motion on sprite**: This block measures how much the video image is moving under the sprite. You can use the menu in it to detect video direction instead of motion, and to detect video on the entire Stage instead of a sprite. It gives a percentage number, so you can adjust the sensitivity by requiring a lower number (to make the program more sensitive) or a higher number (to make it less sensitive to movement).

- **When video motion > 10**: Use this block to trigger a script when video motion is detected.

When you use the webcam or microphone with Scratch, you'll receive a warning. This is to protect your privacy and stop programs and websites from using the webcam without your permission. Click Allow to let Scratch use them.

165

Hot tip

In older versions of Scratch, these blocks were among the Sensing blocks. If you're wondering where they went, add the extension shown below!

Video Sensing
Sense motion with the camera.

You can achieve an interesting effect by putting the pen down on the sprite that's moving. The line it draws seems to be between you and the sprite. Use it as the basis of an interactive art project.

166

Using video direction

Here's a simple game called Donut Chaser that shows how you can use the video direction on a sprite to control it. The Video Sensing blocks are new to you, but the rest of the program should hold no surprises if you've read the earlier chapters.

1 Check you have added the Video Sensing extension. Use the button in the bottom left of the Blocks Palette to add it if not

2 Add a sprite to crawl around the screen. I've used a bug because that looks natural crawling over the screen in all directions

Ladybug1

3 Add this script to your sprite. It works like this: After turning the video on and setting it to fill the screen with no backdrop showing through (0% transparency), we put the sprite in the middle of the screen. We then start a **forever** loop. This checks whether there is video motion on the sprite, and uses a fairly high sensitivity for this. If there is, it points the sprite in the direction of the motion and moves it 20 steps

I used 20 steps in the beetle's movement here because the sprite needs to be able to move at the same speed as my hand, and this felt right. Experiment to see what works well for you, depending on your webcam setup and how fast you move your hand.

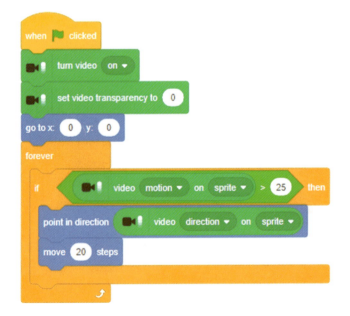

4 Add a sprite to be the target. I chose the donut. Give it the script below

5 Click the green flag to play. When you run the program, you can nudge the sprite around the screen using your hand. The goal is to steer the beetle to the donut, which will then disappear and reappear in a random position

6 There's lots you can do to build on this simple game. You could add a score that increases with each munched donut, add a time limit, or make the donut move around

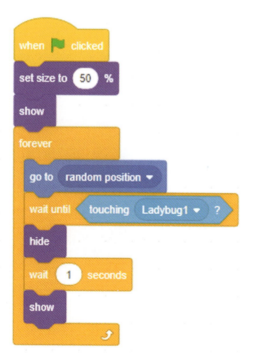

Hot tip

Face the flat or back of your hand to the camera. It makes it easier for the camera to detect your hand movements, and makes the program work better as a result.

Going Batty

There's nothing like a nice peaceful walk, but with all these bats flying around, it's hard to enjoy it. Wave your hands to shoo them away. You'll have to keep at it, though, because they keep coming back!

Going Batty demonstrates video motion on a sprite. It also provides another example of sprite cloning, which you learned about in Chapter 4:

Hot tip

I've set the video sensitivity quite low on this: you need at least 90% motion on the sprite to shoo it away. It takes quite a lot of vigorous hand waving to get rid of the bats! Using low sensitivity works well here, but in most programs, you'll want to use a lower value for the amount of video motion required.

1 Delete the cat sprite. We don't need it for this project

2 Add the Forest backdrop. You can experiment with others, but backdrops with too much detail don't work well

3 Add the Bat2 sprite. It has two costumes that make the bat flap its wings when you switch between them

4 Add this script to the bat to turn the video on and set the transparency so the backdrop and player can both be seen. The bat hides itself because this sprite doesn't move: its clones do. The script then enters a **forever** loop that makes clones of the bat, with a quarter of a second between each one. At a rate of four bats per second, it won't be long before the air is thick with them!

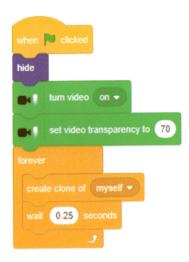

5 Add the script below to the bat. When each clone is created, it is pointed in a random direction, set to a random size (between 50% and 100%), and shown on the Stage. The motion works in a similar way to the beachballs you used in Chapter 4: the bats keep moving forwards, and use the **if on edge, bounce** block to change direction when they reach the edge of the Stage. The loop also continuously checks for video motion on the sprite. If it's above 90%, the clone is deleted. If not, the loop keeps moving the sprite and checking for movement

The blocks related to cloning are all Control blocks. Click the Control button beside the Blocks Palette to find them.

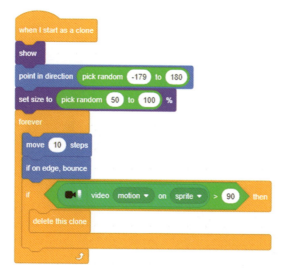

6 Finally, add this script to the bat sprite to make it flap its wings. There are four costumes on the sprite, but only the first two are needed for the flying animation. This script switches between them continuously

Add the Video Sensing extension before creating this script.

To find the "y position of Frank" block, use the "backdrop# of Stage" block. Change Stage to your sprite (Frank in my case) and then change backdrop# to y position. This block can also detect a sprite's x position, size, direction and costume.

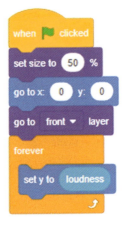

Making a clap-o-meter

There is a Sensing block called **loudness** that is used to detect how loud the sound is if you have a microphone connected. The **loudness** block gives you a percentage. If you don't have a microphone, you can connect some earbuds to the microphone socket on your computer and use them instead.

Here's a script for a clap-o-meter. It turns the loudness value (which will be between 1 and 100) into the sprite's y position. The louder you clap, the higher the sprite climbs.

1 The clap-o-meter works with any sprite. I'm using Frank from the Fantasy category. Add this script to your sprite

2 If you want to keep a record of the highest position reached, add the script below to another sprite. There's a Sensing block that can detect the x or y position of another sprite, so we use that here to check the y position of Frank. If Frank is higher, this sprite goes to its position. As a result, this sprite will always be at the highest point the clap-o-meter sprite has reached. For the movement, use the **go to random position** block and choose Frank in the block's menu

You can use the checkbox beside the "loudness" block to see its value on the Stage.

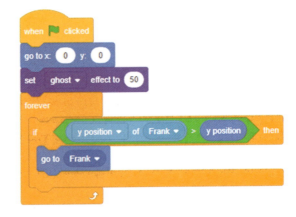

Using a Sense HAT

The Sense HAT was created to carry out experiments on the International Space Station. It sits on top of a Raspberry Pi computer and adds motion and atmospheric sensors as well as an 8x8 grid of multicolored lights (LEDs). It's a great way to add a physical dimension to your Scratch projects.

To access the Sense HAT in Scratch, you need to use the desktop version of Scratch 3, not the online version. You'll find the desktop version of Scratch 3 in the Programming category of your Programs Menu when it's installed. You'll also need to add the Sense HAT extension blocks in Scratch.

LED blocks

There are several blocks that are used to control the LEDs.

- **display text Hello!**: Scrolls a message across the display.

- **display character A**: Shows and keeps a letter on the display.

- **display [pattern]**: Displays a pattern you define on the LED grid.

- **clear display**: Turns all the LEDs off.

- **set colour to [color]**: Sets the color used for your patterns and text.

- **set background to**: Sets the color used for the background of the display.

- **set pixel x:0 y:0 to [color]**: Pixels are numbered from 0 to 7 on the x and y axis. You can individually set any one to any color.

- **set rotation to 0 degrees**: Enables you to rotate the display. Useful if your Pi is mounted sideways or upside down but you don't want to twist your neck reading the display.

Hot tip

The display block enables you to create your own light patterns. The two buttons underneath the grid are used to turn all the lights in the pattern on or off.

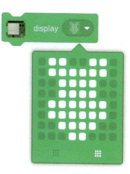

Beware

The Sense HAT shines brightly when you switch your Raspberry Pi on. Don't look into it while powering up.

...cont'd

Movement blocks

There are several blocks that
are used for movement.

- **when joystick pushed up**:
  Starts a script when the
  Sense HAT's joystick is
  pushed up. Choose other
  directions in the block's
  menu. There is also a
  center option for if the
  joystick is pressed down
  in the middle.

- **joystick pushed up**: Test whether the joystick is in a
  particular position or whether the center is pressed down. Use
  this block with an **if**, or **repeat until** block, for example.

- **when shaken**: Starts a script when the Sense HAT is shaken.

- **when tilted forward**: Starts a script when the Sense HAT is
  tilted in a particular direction. Each tilt starts the script once.
  If you tilt the Raspberry Pi forward and leave it there, the
  script only starts once.

Right: The Sense HAT
mounted on a Raspberry
Pi. The joystick is at the
bottom, to the right of
the Raspberry Pi logo.

Sensor blocks

There are several blocks you can use to read the sensors. They have checkboxes you can use to display their values on the Stage.

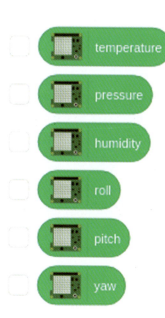

- **temperature**: Measures temperature in Celsius.

- **pressure**: Gives you the air pressure. Could be used for experiments at high altitude, for example.

- **humidity**: Tells you how much water vapor is in the air as a percentage.

- **roll**: Hold your Raspberry Pi flat, with the Sense HAT facing up and its LED grid on the left. If you tilt your Raspberry Pi towards you or away from you, this is the roll motion. Sensor values go from 0 to (nearly) 360. The flat position is 0 or 360. As you turn it towards you, it counts up from 0, and if you turn it in a full circle it will reach 360.

- **pitch**: Holding the Raspberry Pi flat once more, the pitch motion is when you rock the left or right side up or down. Values for this are less intuitive. The flat position is 0. If you tilt counter clockwise, values go from 0 to 90, and then from 90 back to 0 again when the Pi is upside down. Turning clockwise, values go from 360 (flat) to 270 when turned through 90 degrees, and from 270 to 360 again when the Pi is upside down.

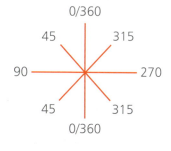

- **yaw**: If you put your Raspberry Pi flat on a desk and spin it around, that is the yaw motion. It behaves like a compass, and gives you the number of degrees from north.

Beware

The reading for the temperature is affected by the temperature of the Sense HAT itself.

Hot tip

To understand the movements, check the boxes beside roll, pitch and yaw in the Blocks Palette and then move the Sense HAT around. Watch how the numbers change.

Hot tip

I've told you which way to hold your Raspberry Pi to help explain these movements, but you can hold the Pi other ways. You can hold it with the Sense HAT facing you and rock it left and right like a steering wheel (pitch), or spin it around upside down (yaw).

It's a good idea to use a case on your Raspberry Pi with the Sense HAT. Choose a case that protects the Raspberry Pi board but gives you access to the GPIO pins so you can fit the Sense HAT. I use the Pibow Coupé from Pimoroni.

Don't forget

Add the Sense HAT extension so you can find the blocks you'll need for this game.

Raspberry Pi Sense HAT
Control Raspberry Pi Sense HAT

Collaboration with
Raspberry Pi

Introducing Feeding Time

Here's a game you can create for the Sense HAT, called Feeding Time. You're the zookeeper at a dinosaur park, and the dinos are getting hungry. It's your job to feed them. As you might guess, the only safe way to feed a dinosaur is from a distance!

Tilt the Raspberry Pi forwards, backwards, left or right to move the Scratch cat around the Stage. Use the joystick to fire a donut at a dinosaur, either left, right, up or down. When you feed a dinosaur, it goes away.

Keep clear of the dinos to avoid sapping your energy. The game ends when your energy reaches 0, or there are 30 dinosaurs on the screen roaring for food. In either case, you've failed in your task.

In this project you'll see how to:

● Use the Sense HAT to enable tilt controls in Scratch.

● Detect joystick movements.

● Display a message on the LED grid.

● Flash colors on the LED grid.

This project will use cloning for the dinosaurs, and will give you movement controls you can reuse in other games.

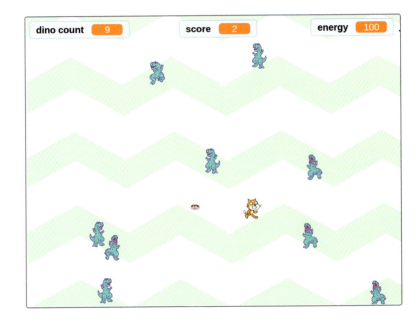

Creating the cat's script

Add this script to your cat sprite. When you've created it, click the **green flag** button and tilt the Pi to move the cat.

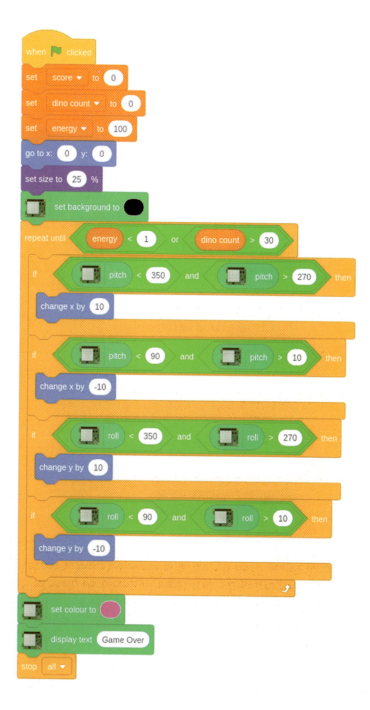

You'll need to make the variables *dino count*, *energy* and *score* to build this script. Leave them checked in the Blocks Palette and arrange them on the Stage so players can check their progress.

The movement instructions require the device to be tilted by more than 10 degrees. For example, pitch values of 0 to 10 (slight tilt left) or 350 to 360 (slight tilt right) do not move the cat. It would get irritating if you couldn't keep the cat still.

This script shows how to scroll a message too: when the game ends, the LED grid displays "Game Over".

Adding the donut scripts

 Add the donut sprite. You'll find it in the Food category

Donut

 Click the **My Blocks** button beside the Blocks Palette. Make a block and call it "fire donut"

3 Add this script to your donut sprite. It detects joystick movements and uses them to fire the donut

176

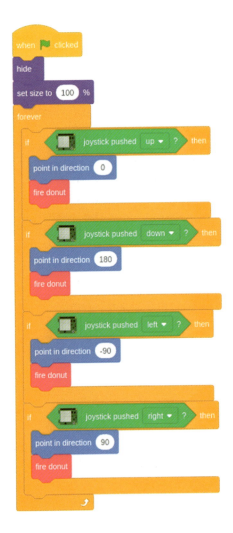

4 Add the sprite Dinosaur5. I've chosen this one because it has some nice costumes for the animation. You're adding it now because the next script will refer to it

Dinosaur5

Don't forget

The "define fire donut" block was added for you when you made that block. You'll find it in the Code Area.

5 Click the **donut** sprite in the Sprite List. The next script goes on the donut, not the dinosaur you just added

6 Add the script below to your donut sprite. This moves the donut to the player sprite (Sprite1) and then moves it across the Stage until it reaches a dinosaur or the edge of the Stage. It then disappears

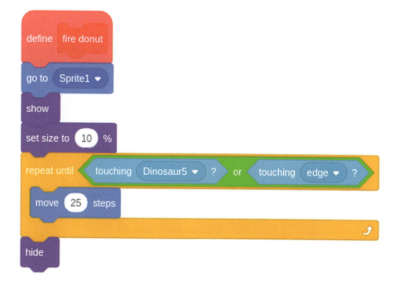

Hot tip

The "touching?" block can be used to detect any clone of that sprite. Here, it's detecting any clone of the dinosaur.

7 Click the **green flag**. You can now test moving in four directions by tilting, and firing donuts in four directions using the joystick. Check the donut disappears when it hits the dinosaur, or the edge of the Stage

177

Adding the dinosaur scripts

1 Click the dinosaur sprite in the Sprite List

2 Add the script on the right to the dinosaur. It endlessly creates dinosaur clones. Only the clones will move, so this original sprite is hidden

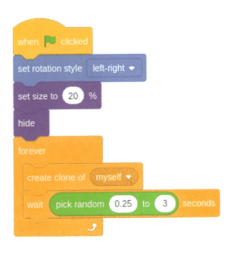

3 Add the script below to your dinosaur sprite. Each clone starts at the edge of the screen, glides to the player and then does its hungry stomping animation endlessly

4 Give the dino this script. It checks whether the dino is touching the donut or the player. If it's touching a donut, the clone is deleted. If it's touching the player, the energy variable is reduced. Now click the **green flag** to play!

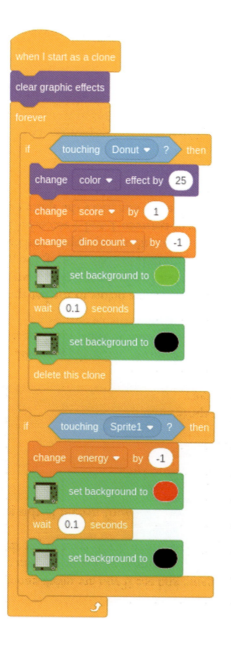

Hot tip

This script makes the Sense HAT flash green when the player feeds the dino successfully, and red when their energy is sapped. A quick way to do that is to set the background color.

Hot tip

If you find the game too easy, you can try changing the energy by -5 when the player touches a dinosaur.

179

Don't forget

The *dino count* variable keeps track of how many dinosaurs are on screen. It goes up when a new dino is cloned, and goes down when a dino goes away because it's been fed. The game ends if there are 30 dinos needing feeding.

To use a micro:bit with Scratch you need a computer that supports Bluetooth. That's how the computer and the micro:bit communicate, once the software has been installed.

At the time of writing, the micro:bit doesn't work with Scratch on the Raspberry Pi. There are plans to update the Scratch 3 desktop software to enable it to be used in the future.

If you have a battery pack, you can disconnect the micro:bit from the USB cable as soon as you've installed the software over it.

Setting up a micro:bit

The micro:bit is a board that plugs into your computer by USB and can be easily battery powered. It's affordable (at under £15 or $19), and adds motion sensors, two buttons, and a grid of 5x5 red lights (LEDs). You can use it to hook up simple switches, too.

To set up the micro:bit, follow these steps:

 Install the Scratch Link software. You can find it at **https://scratch.mit.edu/microbit**

 You need to install some software on the micro:bit. Download the HEX file, also at **https://scratch.mit.edu/microbit**. Connect your micro:bit to your computer using a USB cable, and then drag and drop the HEX file onto your micro:bit device. It's just the same as copying a file between folders on your computer, or copying them to a USB key. Your micro:bit scrolls its name across its LEDs so you can identify it

 In the Scratch editor, click the **Add Extension** button in the bottom left of the Blocks Palette. Choose the micro:bit extension

 You'll be able to see any available devices to connect to and can choose yours

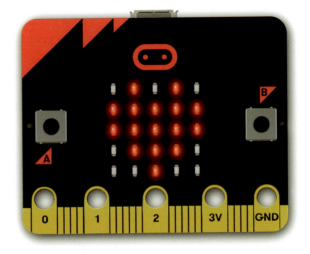

Using a micro:bit

There are several blocks that are used to control the micro:bit.

- **when A button pressed**: This block triggers a script when the **A** (left) button, **B** (right) button, or either button is pressed.

- **A button pressed?**: Used to check whether a button is pressed. Choose which button (or choose any button) in the menu.

- **when moved**: Starts a script when the micro:bit is moved, shaken or jumped.

- **display [pattern]**: Displays a pattern you define on the 5x5 grid of red LEDs.

- **display text Hello!**: Scrolls a message across the micro:bit's LED grid.

- **clear display**: Turns all the lights off.

- **when tilted [direction]**: Starts a script when the device is tilted to the front, back, left or right, or in any direction.

- **tilted any?**: Checks whether the unit is tilted in any direction, or in a direction you choose.

- **tilt angle front**: Gives you the angle of tilt on a scale of 0 to 100. A tilt in the opposite direction gives a negative number. You can choose other directions in the block's menu.

- **when pin 0 connected**: Starts a script when a circuit is connected to pin 0. Scratch enables you to connect to the large pins 0, 1 and 2, which can be used with crocodile clips.

Don't forget

If your device becomes disconnected, you can go to the micro:bit section of the Blocks Palette and click the orange alert button to reconnect.

Hot tip

To connect a circuit, try putting a wire between one of the numbered pins and the GND pin. You can make a simple switch in between. I connected foldback clips to the numbered pins, and tinfoil to GND so I could make a circuit by flicking the clips down.

Hot tip

You could add scores into this game, perhaps based on survival time (using an energy meter) or levels cleared. This demo simply makes a popping sound if you touch the floor or ceiling, and draws a new cave when you get to the right of the screen.

Hot tip

There is no checkbox beside the micro:bit blocks to display values on the Stage. Use a script like this to experiment with tilt values.

Introducing Balloon Floater

This game is like the fairground attraction where you have to move a loop along a twisted wire without touching the wire.

In Balloon Floater, you have to guide a balloon through a cave, without touching the jaggedy floor or ceiling. While it is possible to play the game using a keyboard, it's more challenging to use the micro:bit to control the balloon's speed and direction.

You tilt the micro:bit forward to move the balloon up, and back to move it down. Tilt left and right to move in those directions. Unlike other games we've made in this book, the balloon in this one has momentum. Your movements change the balloon's speed in the up/down or left/right directions, rather than just moving it a certain number of steps. If it's going up too fast, for example, tilt back to slow it down.

To make it easier, you can press button **A** to brake, or **B** to dash to the end if you're lined up with the exit.

In this project you'll see how to:

● Use the micro:bit tilt controls to move a sprite.

● Use the buttons on the micro:bit to start a script.

● Show patterns on the micro:bit's LEDs.

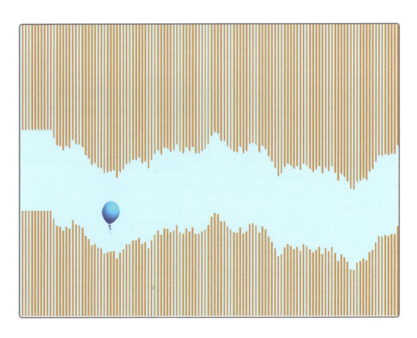

Drawing the cave

First, let's draw the cave that the balloon must float through.

1 Delete the cat. Add a sprite to draw the cave. I chose the pencil

Pencil

2 Click the **Variables** button beside the Blocks Palette and create a new variable called *corridor y position*

3 Click the **My Blocks** button beside the Blocks Palette and make a block called "draw line"

4 Add the script below to your sprite. It draws one line in the cave. It starts at the bottom of the Stage, draws a line to where the corridor begins, lifts the pen, goes up 100 steps, then draws another line to the top of the Stage

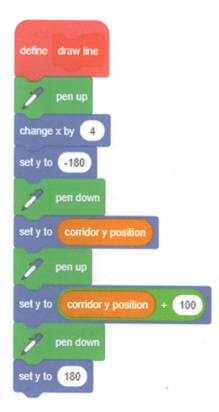

Don't forget

You need to add the Pen extension so you can use the Pen blocks.

Don't forget

The "define" block is added in the Code Area when you make a block. You can't find it in the Blocks Palette.

183

Hot tip

The micro:bit is lightweight, small and can be powered from two AAA batteries. That makes it ideal for using with toys. You could attach it to a teddy bear and make the bear squeal with joy when it's thrown in the air, for example.

...cont'd

Hot tip

The corridor draws 10 straight lines before the passage starts to turn, so there's a safe space for the balloon at the start of each level. Otherwise, my testing found the balloon can start the level touching the cave, which is unfair on the player.

Hot tip

Each line can be up to 10 steps higher or lower than the previous one. The script makes sure the corridor doesn't get too close to the top or bottom of the Stage by enforcing maximum and minimum values. If the value is too big, it's set to the maximum allowed. If it's too small, it's set to the minimum.

5 Drag in a **when I receive new message** block from the Events part of the Blocks Palette. Use the menu in it to create a new message called "draw level"

6 Complete the script with the blocks shown below. Click it to draw the cave

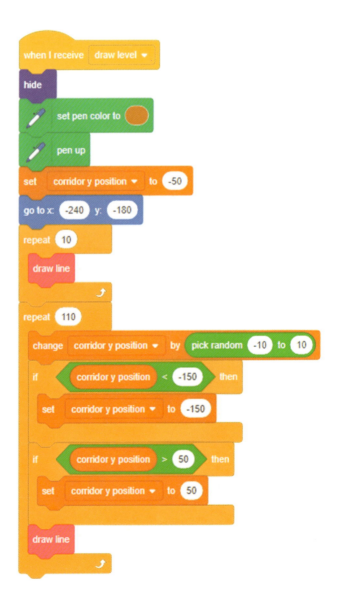

Coding the balloon

Now, let's add the balloon and its code.

1 Add the Balloon1 sprite from the sprite library. The quickest way to find it is to search for it by name

Balloon1

2 Click the **Variables** button and create new variables called *velocity up*, *velocity right*, and *new velocity*

3 Click the **My Blocks** button and make new blocks called "horizontal movement", "vertical movement", and "limit velocity". Add a "number or text" input box called "velocity" to the **limit velocity** block. The others need no input

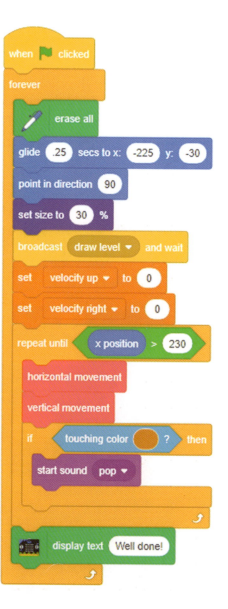

4 Add this script to your balloon. In the **touching color?** block, choose the color from the cave wall drawn on the Stage

185

Don't forget

You need to add the micro:bit extension whenever you want to use the micro:bit blocks.

micro:bit
Connect your projects with the world.

Requires   Collaboration with
                    micro:bit

...cont'd

Don't forget

Velocity is speed combined with the direction of motion.

Hot tip

Adding a slight turn movement in the balloon gives it a feeling of floating on the breeze.

Hot tip

Through testing, I found that you get a good feeling of control by using a minimum tilt of 20 degrees and changing the speed by 0.2. You might need to experiment to find the right degree of tilt and amount of movement for your own projects.

5 Add the script below to your balloon sprite. In this game, the vertical and horizontal speed are managed separately. When you tilt right, the velocity to the right goes up by 0.2 steps. When you tilt left, it goes down by 0.2 steps. To actually move the balloon left, you can tilt until the velocity to the right is negative. Whether or not you change the speed, each time this script runs, the balloon drifts left or right by the number of steps in the *velocity right* variable. The minimum movement is a single step, so Scratch will round the number of steps up or down when the velocity is a decimal value (such as 0.2)

...cont'd

Hot tip

If you don't have a micro:bit, you can make this game work with the keyboard. For example, replace the "tilt angle front > 20" blocks with the "key [up arrow] pressed?" Sensing block. Delete the scripts for the A and B buttons, and the "display text" block.

6 The vertical movement uses a similar script. Add it now

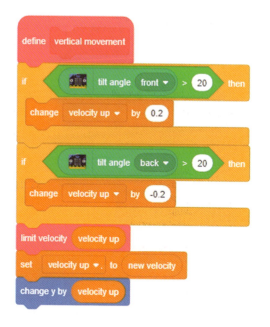

7 Finally, the "limit velocity" script is used to stop the velocity being more than 10 or less than -10. It's used by both the horizontal and vertical movement scripts to keep the speed under control. The *new velocity* variable is used to send the new velocity back to the movement script

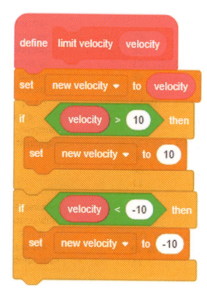

Hot tip

If the velocity is already between -10 and 10, the *new velocity* variable will be the same as the current velocity. That's fine. It doesn't do any harm to set a variable to the value it already is, which is what would happen in the movement script in that case.

Don't forget

Click the pattern in the "display [pattern]" block to edit the pattern. The empty and filled grids at the bottom can be used to turn all the lights on or off in your pattern.

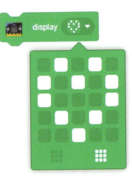

Coding the buttons

We'll add two scripts to the balloon to react to button pushes.

1 Add this script to the balloon to react to button **A** being pressed. It resets both velocity variables, and shows a "stop" sign on the LED display. You'll need to design the stop pattern yourself. After a 1-second pause, the display is cleared

2 The final script in this project reacts to button **B** being pressed. It sets the *velocity right* variable to 20, which is double the maximum you can achieve with tilt controls. It makes the balloon dash to the right. An arrow shows on the display

Hot tip

Now you're ready to play the game. Take care not to press the reset button on the underside of your micro:bit as you hold it.

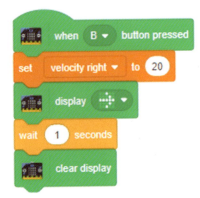

Using the Raspberry Pi GPIO

The Raspberry Pi has a series of pins in the top-left corner of the board, on its top surface, called General Purpose Input/Output pins (GPIO pins). These pins can be used to connect your own electronics projects to the Raspberry Pi, which you can then control using software.

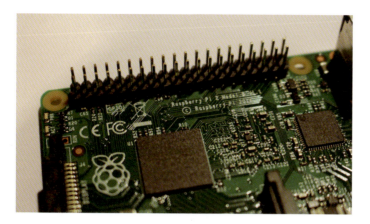

1 For this project, you will need a light emitting diode (LED), and a resistor of at least 330 ohm. If you don't have a single resistor of that value, you can join two lower-value resistors together end to end to add up to at least 330 ohm

2 An LED has a long leg and a short leg. At the base of the LED's dome, it is flat above the short leg, so you can tell them apart even after you've separated them

3 Gently bend the LED's legs apart and connect your resistor to the long leg of your LED. If you don't know how to solder, you can do this by just twisting the resistor's wire around the LED's leg

Beware

Don't connect things to the GPIO pins unless you know what you're doing. You could break your Raspberry Pi.

Hot tip

It's okay to connect your LED and resistor while the Raspberry Pi is switched on, but usually you should switch off your Raspberry Pi before connecting something to the GPIO pins.

Hot tip

An LED is a component that lights up and that only allows electrical current to pass through it in one direction. A resistor is a component that limits the amount of current going through a circuit. In this project, it's here to protect the Raspberry Pi.

...cont'd

Raspberry Pi GPIO
Control Raspberry Pi GPIO lines

Collaboration with
Raspberry Pi

4 Connect a female-to-female jumper wire to one leg of the LED and another to the other end of your resistor

5 Position your Raspberry Pi so the logo on the top is the right way up. For the purposes of this example, forget about the top row of pins. Your resistor wire goes on the 6th pin from the left on the bottom row. The other wire goes on the 13th pin from the left on the bottom row. So there should be 5 unused pins, your resistor wire, 6 unused pins and then your other wire connected to the Raspberry Pi

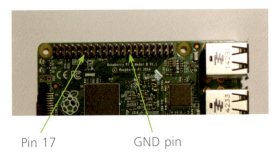

Pin 17   GND pin

6 Now you're connected, you can use Scratch to control your LED. First, add the Raspberry Pi Simple Electronics extension, which includes blocks for using buttons and LEDs connected to your Raspberry Pi

7 The extension has new blocks you can use to turn your LED on and off. The LED is connected to GPIO pin number 17. There's no easy way to work out the pin number: you have to look it up. Try this script, which flashes the LED on and off

10 Seven shorties

To finish up, here are seven short programs you can build and experiment with, including five games, a chat program and an art generator.

Keepy-Uppy

In this game, a cross between football and Pong, you have to keep the ball in play. Each time it hits the wall, it knocks a chunk out. The aim is to get it through the other side of the wall:

1 Delete the cat sprite and add the Jordyn sprite. She's in the Sports category. Add the soccer ball too

2 Add this script to position Jordyn and enable her to move left and right

3 Paint a new backdrop, and fill it with a green rectangle that covers the whole Stage. Add a solid red box across the width of the Stage, but leave room at the top for the ball to get out

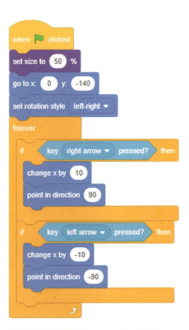

Beware

This game requires keyboard controls to play, so you can't play it on tablet devices.

Hot tip

To make a solid red box without a border, set the Outline color in the Paint Editor to use the transparent ink color.

Don't forget

The Pen blocks are in an extension. Add them using the button at the bottom left of the Blocks Palette.

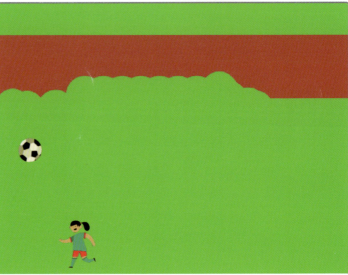

...cont'd

4 Click the ball, and add these scripts to it. Use the My Blocks part of the Blocks Palette to create the blocks for bouncing off the wall and checking whether the game has ended. When you're setting the colors in the **touching color?** and **set pen color** blocks, use the pipette to copy them from the Stage

It looks like the wall is breaking down, but actually you're drawing on top of it in the same color as the backdrop. This game won't work with a patterned backdrop, as a result.

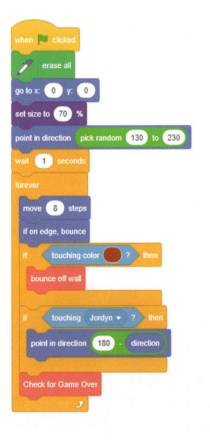

193

To improve this game, you could add a score that increases each time the ball bounces off the girl, and add some randomness in the direction the ball goes after touching the player.

5 You could improve presentation with a title screen, sound effects, and proper winning and losing sequences

Beware

This game requires keyboard controls to play, so you can't play it on tablet devices.

Hot tip

This game is similar to Super Dodgeball, with three moving obstacles and a target to reach. It shows how one game idea can inspire quite different designs. What else can you do with this concept?

Hot tip

If the cars move too fast, use lower numbers in their "move 10 steps" blocks.

Shop Cat

Can you help the cat to cross the road to do its shopping, and then take it home again?

1 Make a variable called *score* for all sprites

2 Add the Night City backdrop, from the Outdoors category

3 Rename your cat sprite to Cat

4 Add one of the vehicle sprites and give it this script

5 Right-click your vehicle sprite in the Sprite List and choose **duplicate** twice, to create two more vehicles

6 Click one of the vehicle sprites, and change the number -65 in the **set y to -65** block to -108. This puts that vehicle on the lower lane of the road. Change the speed of the duplicate vehicles too by editing the number of steps moved in the script from 10 to 15 and 12

```
when [flag] clicked
set size to (40) %
go to x: (0) y: (-150)
point in direction (90)
forever
  if < key [up arrow ▼] pressed? > then
    change y by (10)
    next costume
  if < key [down arrow ▼] pressed? > then
    change y by (-10)
    next costume
  if < key [left arrow ▼] pressed? > then
    change x by (-10)
    next costume
  if < key [right arrow ▼] pressed? > then
    change x by (10)
    next costume
```

7 You can add other vehicle costumes to the duplicate vehicles. See Chapter 5 for advice on adding costumes

8 Click the cat and add this script (see right) to it

...cont'd

 Add this script to the cat.
When a vehicle hits the cat,
this script ends the game

 Add a new sprite to
represent the shopping.
Add additional costumes
for other shopping items

 Add the following script to your shopping item sprite.
When the cat touches the shopping, the shopping hides
and waits until the cat reaches the bottom of the screen
again before showing the next item

Above: The costumes I
used to represent the
shopping.

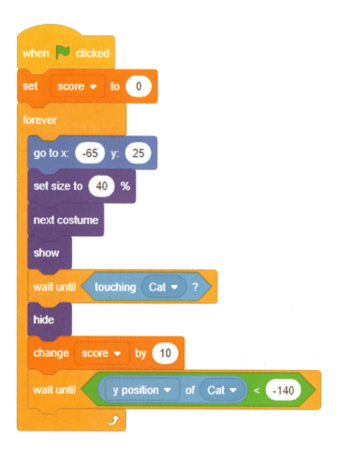

Penguin Patter

In Penguin Patter, you can chat to a friendly penguin:

1 Delete the cat. Add a backdrop and sprite. I've used the sprite Penguin 2 and Beach Malibu backdrop

2 Make the variable *random choice* and the list *sayings*. They can be for all sprites. Uncheck the boxes in the Blocks Palette to hide them

3 Add this script to your sprite. You'll need to add the Text to Speech extension for the **speak** block

Above: You type in what you want to say. The penguin's replies appear on screen and are also spoken out loud.

```
when [flag] clicked
set voice to (squeak ▾)
delete (all) of (sayings ▾)
add (What do you mean by that?) to (sayings ▾)
add (Tell me more!) to (sayings ▾)
add (Really?) to (sayings ▾)
add (My favourite food is fish. What about you?) to (sayings ▾)
add (I love swimming!) to (sayings ▾)
speak (What shall we talk about?)
ask (What shall we talk about?) and wait
forever
    set (random choice ▾) to (pick random (1) to (length of (sayings ▾)))
    speak (item (random choice) of (sayings ▾))
    ask (item (random choice) of (sayings ▾)) and wait
    replace item (random choice) of (sayings ▾) with (answer)
    next costume
```

Hot tip

I used a variable to remember which saying was randomly chosen, so the program can replace it with what the player enters. As a result, the penguin learns what you say and copies you.

Hot tip

Customize this game with your own personality. You can add lots more sayings at the start, and the program works better the more you add.

Abstract Artist

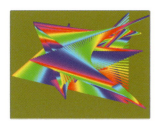

Above: Abstract art!

Unleash the creative genius in your computer with Abstract Artist, a program that makes a random, continuously changing artwork:

1 Start a new project and add the script below to your cat sprite. It makes the cat glide to random points on the screen, while hidden

Hot tip

You can make very different artworks by changing how the invisible cats move across the Stage, by adding in other sprites that the painting sprite can hop between, or by adjusting how the colors and pen shades change.

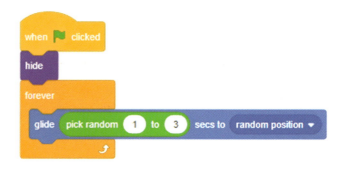

2 Right-click the cat sprite in the Sprite List and click **duplicate**. Now there are two invisible, prowling cats

3 Paint a new backdrop, and fill it with a solid dark color, to make the brightly colored art really pop out

4 Add a new sprite (it doesn't matter which) and give it the second script on this page. The script makes it flit between the two invisible cats, drawing a line in a new color each time

Don't forget

Before you can use the Pen blocks you need to add the Pen extension. Use the button in the bottom left of the Blocks Palette.

198

Maze Mania

This simple script enables you to play a maze, and keeps you honest by stopping you from walking through the walls. You can draw your maze as a Stage backdrop or a sprite costume. I created mine using Maze Generator (**www.mazegenerator.net**), with dimensions of 30 by 20, and then imported that as a sprite costume. All your walls need to be the same color. To stop your sprite snagging on walls, use a round sprite:

1 Position your maze so it fits on the Stage. I had to set mine to 97% size, and put it at x:0 y:0

2 Create new variables, called *old x* and *old y*

3 Add the script shown here to the sprite that will move through the maze. I used one of the ball sprites. Use the pipette to choose the color of the walls in the **touching color?** block

4 Set your sprite's starting position and adjust the size of your sprite in the script to make it fit comfortably between the walls

This game requires keyboard controls to play, so you can't play it on tablet devices.

If you're drawing your own maze, use the line drawing tools to keep your lines straight.

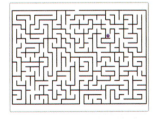

Above: The maze game in action. Can purple blob escape?

Hot tip

This game uses a "wait until" block to wait for 20 seconds before ending the game (see facing page). There's also a hat block you can use to start scripts after a certain time. It's an Events block called "when loudness > 10", and it has a menu so you can start scripts instead when the timer reaches a certain number.

Hot tip

Your scripts might appear on top of each other when you copy them to other sprites. Right-click the Code Area and choose Clean Up Blocks to tidy them up.

Photo Safari

Go on safari in this game and see if you are quick enough to be a wildlife photographer. The animals appear at random times, and you have to be quick to click them if you want to get that shot!

1 Delete the cat sprite. You won't need it in this game

2 Add a nature backdrop from the Outdoors category

3 Add the Bat sprite from the Animals category

4 Click the **Variables** button and make a variable called *score*. Leave its box checked to show it on the Stage

5 Add the two simple scripts below to the bat sprite. The first one hides the bat (ready for the game start), puts it in the top left and shrinks it to 75%. During the game, the script makes the bat continuously appear and disappear at random intervals of between 1 and 4 seconds. The second script increases the score and hides the sprite when it is clicked

6 Import five more animal sprites. Copy the scripts from your bat to them. To copy a script, click the bat sprite in the Sprite List, and drag the script from its Code Area over another sprite in the Sprite List. When you release the mouse button, your script is copied across to that sprite

7 Go into each sprite and adjust the x and y position in the script, so the animals are spread around the screen. I put a frog at x:162 y:-125; a ladybug at x:25 y:-65; a butterfly at x:-155 y:-130; a parrot at x:130 y:85; and a hedgehog at x:-100 y:0

You can adjust the score too. Animals that are smaller (harder to click!) or aren't on screen for as long should award a higher score than others!

8 Change the random numbers used in the script of each sprite depending on how often you want it to appear. The **wait** block *after* the **show** block determines how long it's shown for. The other **wait** block decides how long it's hidden for

The game is timed to last 20 seconds, but you could extend that in the Game Over script.

9 Create a new sprite that says Game Over. I made mine in Word so I could use a funky font. I pressed the Print Screen key, pasted into Paint, and then saved the image

10 Add this script (right) to the Game Over sprite to complete the game

Above: The Stage when the game ends.

Gran Ama's Anagrams Quiz

Hot tip

"Gran Ama" is an anagram of "anagram"!

In this game, you're challenged to decode scrambled words, or anagrams. You can customize the game with themed lists of words, such as foods, places or characters from books.

1 Delete the cat sprite and add the Wanda sprite

2 Change the backdrop to one of the stage images

3 Click the **Variables** button and make these variables: *counter*, *letter*, *score*, *word length*, *scrambled word*, and *word to scramble*. Clear the boxes beside all of these variables in the Blocks Palette, except for *score*. Drag the score box on the Stage to one of the corners

4 In the Variables part of the Blocks Palette, you also need to create two lists: *letters* and *words*

Hot tip

There's nothing to stop the same word coming around twice, but that's less likely with a longer list. The nice thing is that the same words lead to different questions because the anagrams are randomly generated.

5 In the box for the *words* list on the Stage, click the + button and type in a list of words. When you've finished, clear the boxes beside these lists in the Blocks Palette to hide them from the Stage. The more words you add to your list, the less likely it is that words will repeat during a game

6 Click the **My Blocks** button beside the Blocks Palette. Click the button to **Make a Block**, and call it "scramble". It doesn't need any inputs or labels

7 Add the script below to your Wanda sprite. This is the main game loop that asks you to unscramble five words, tells you if you're right or not and keeps score. In the **join** blocks, put a space at the end of the first piece of text (such as "No! The answer was ") to ensure the answer doesn't join up without a gap

Hot tip

You can import a file into a list. For example, you could bring in a list of words from a text editor, where each word is on a new line. To import a file, right-click on the list's box on the Stage.

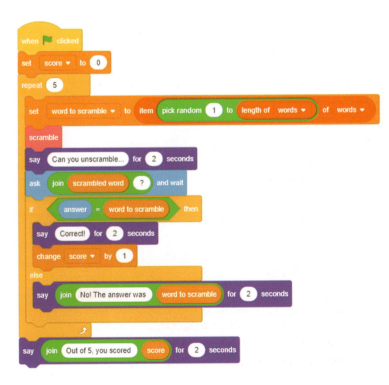

...cont'd

The scrambling code includes a safety check to make sure the jumbled-up word isn't coincidentally the same as the original word. That can happen otherwise from time to time with this program!

This script uses the "not" Operator block. Usually, in an "if" or "repeat until" block you run some blocks if or until something you're checking is true. The "not" block reverses that, so you can run some blocks if something is *not* true. This script uses the "not" block to keep creating new scrambled words until the result is different to the original word.

8 Add the script on this page, which scrambles a word. It breaks the letters into a list called *letters*. Then it scrambles the list by putting the first letter in a random place in the list, 10 times. Then the variable *scrambled word* is made by joining all the letters from the jumbled-up *letters* list

11 Making and sharing projects

Now it's time to make your own projects! Discover tips and resources to help here.

Making your own programs

Now you've seen how programs are built in Scratch, you can start to design and share your own creations. Here are some tips:

1 It's rare to program something that works first time unless it's a really simple program. Programming is all about trying something out, testing it, and then changing your scripts. Keep testing your program as you build it. You can click a script in the Code Area to run it straight away without running your whole program

2 If you need to reset the position or look of a sprite for testing, remember you can click blocks in the Blocks Palette to use them on your sprite straight away

3 If you're having problems with a variable, click the checkbox beside it in the Variables part of the Blocks Palette. That will show the variable's value on the Stage so you can see what's going on. You can also show the x and y coordinates and direction of a sprite by checking the boxes beside them in the Motion blocks

4 If you can't see all the blocks, check whether you need to add an extension. Extension blocks have an icon on them and can be added using the **Add Extension** button in the bottom left of the Blocks Palette

5 To tidy up the Code Area, right-click on it and then choose Clean up Blocks from the menu. This lines up all your scripts and stops them overlapping

6 Add comments to your script to help you to remember what it's doing, and what you need to do with it next. Right-click on the Code Area to add a comment box. Click the bottom-right corner to resize it, and drag it into the Blocks Palette to delete it

Scripts glow in the Code Area as they run.

A great way to start making your own projects is by modifying existing projects. How can you build on the projects in this book?

Fixing common errors

Every project is different, but there are a few bugs that come up more often than others:

- If your program isn't repeating things correctly, or isn't making decisions it should, check your Control blocks. When you have a complicated program, it's easy to end up with something inside the wrong bracket, but this completely changes the meaning of the program. Compare the two scripts below, and the shapes they create (shape pictures are not to the same scale):

Errors in programs are often called "bugs".

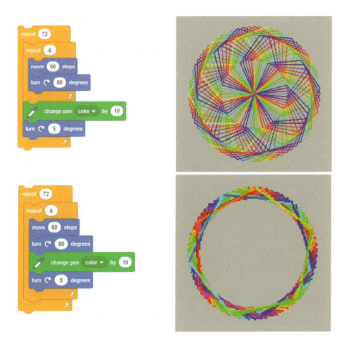

As you try to fix your program, you might make it worse! Save a copy of it so you can always go back to the previous version later (see page 20 in Chapter 1).

- If a sprite sticks at the edge of the screen, check that you're not changing its coordinates to a position that is off the screen.

- Whenever you write a script, select the right sprite in the Sprite List first. If you need to copy a script from one sprite to another, click the script in the Code Area and drag it onto the other sprite in the Sprite List.

- If you have an error that only occurs sometimes, check your variables and any blocks using random numbers.

Try reading your program aloud, or following its instructions with pen and paper. It can help you to spot problems with blocks being in the wrong order, or the wrong blocks being used together.

...cont'd

Beware

Remember to change the numbers or menu options in blocks when you add them to your scripts.

Beware

You can't divide a number by zero, so it will cause an error if you try.

Hot tip

If you have problems with sprites not being synchronized with each other, use broadcasts (see page 103 in Chapter 6).

● Take care with lookalike blocks. It's easy to mix up the **set** and **change** blocks used with positions or variables, or the **broadcast** and **broadcast and wait** blocks.

● Be careful with the order of blocks. In particular, make sure you don't accidentally reset a variable's value (using the **set [variable name] to 0** block) after you've started using it to store information.

● When you're comparing two pieces of text, Scratch won't think they're the same if there are extra spaces in one of them. This script won't work as expected because of the extra spaces after "YES".

● If your program works first time but doesn't work after that, it might be because your program isn't set up correctly when it begins. Position the sprites where they should be, make them visible and set their direction. Set your variables to their starting values too. Make sure that no changes made in the previous run remain.

● There is a Turbo mode you can use to run your program extremely fast. It can help you to identify problems with programs that take a long time to run. Hold down the Shift key and click the green flag to turn Turbo mode on or off. You can also enable it from the Edit menu.

● To track down a bug in a script, you can also try breaking it down into smaller pieces by stopping it early. You can use a Control block to stop the script, other scripts on the same sprite, or all scripts on all sprites at any point in the program. You can then inspect the values of variables at that point by showing them on the Stage, to help you work out what's going on.

Sharing your projects

There's a strong community for Scratch, built around sharing projects and feedback on them. When you share a project, you enable anyone to play it on the Scratch website, and also give them permission to modify it and share their versions of it.

Each project in Scratch has a project page (shown at the bottom of this page). It provides information about the project and enables people to run it. You can go to a project page by clicking a project's thumbnail in the My Stuff part of your profile.

To share a project, click one of the **Share** buttons. You can find one at the top of the editor, and another on the project page.

When you click the button, your project is shared and you are taken to its project page. Add instructions, and notes and credits. If you use someone else's work in your project, thank them here.

To see all the comments on your project, visit its project page on the Scratch website. You can find it by clicking your username in the top right and then clicking **My Stuff**. You'll also see message notifications at the top of the Scratch website (but not in the editor where it might distract you!).

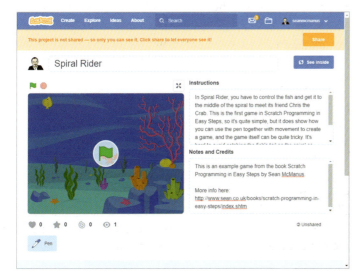

Don't forget to leave feedback for others too. Click Explore at the top of the website to find projects and leave your comments under the project player.

To unshare a project, click your profile name in the top right, go to My Stuff, then click the Unshare link beside the project.

209

Because of copyright law, you're not allowed to use pictures or sounds you find online in the projects you share. The exception is if the person who made them has given you permission.

Also available in this series by the same author: Cool Scratch Projects in easy steps. Build a drum machine, make projects with 3D glasses (included in the print edition), animate cartoon frogs, code maze games, and more!

If you enjoyed this book, please blog about it or write a review of it on your favorite online store! Thank you!

Resources & Thank yous

The Scratch website
https://scratch.mit.edu/

The author's website, including examples, links to find the projects in this book online, and bonus content
https://www.sean.co.uk/scratch

Scratch Wiki: a reference guide to Scratch
https://en.scratch-wiki.info/wiki/Scratch_Wiki

Raspberry Pi forums, including one dedicated to Scratch
http://www.raspberrypi.org/forums/

To download the examples in this book, visit **www.ineasysteps.com** Select **Free Resources** and then choose **Downloads**.

Acknowledgements

Scratch is developed by the Lifelong Kindergarten Group at the MIT Media Lab. See **https://scratch.mit.edu**

Special thanks to Mai T. Vu, J.D. and the students in her programming class at Casey Middle School in Boulder, Colorado; Darrell Little; and Laurence Molloy, who all helped with testing projects for this updated second edition.

Thank you to everyone who read the first edition and sent such lovely feedback! It's been amazing to see your projects!

Sense HAT photos are courtesy of Raspberry Pi. Image of micro:bit courtesy of micro:bit Educational Foundation at **microbit.org**. Thank you to those who helped with permissions and research queries, including Mitchel Resnick; Liz Upton, Eben Upton, Lucy Hattersley and Helen Lynn of Raspberry Pi; Jan Boström; Tim Benson; and Mike Cook.

Extra special thanks to Karen McManus, who was a fantastic help throughout this project, in particular with indexing and layout into the In Easy Steps style; and to star playtester Leo.

About the author
Sean McManus is an expert technology writer and Scratch enthusiast. He writes for The MagPi magazine and his other books include Cool Scratch Projects in easy steps, Coder Academy, Raspberry Pi For Dummies, and Web Design in easy steps. Visit his website at **www.sean.co.uk** for additional resources.

Index

C